DAYDREAM DISTRACTIONS

An Anthology

Poems, Notations, Short Stories, Excerpts

by

Nathaniel Robert Winters

The Buffalo Publishing Company

of the Napa Valley

First edition

Daydream Distractions

Nathaniel Robert Winters

Table of Contents

Table of Contents-continued

1. Introduction:

You Can Call Me…

"You can't judge a book by its cover." But people buy books by their cover in bookstores all the time. How much can you learn from someone's name or nickname. I've had my name and nicknames evolve over my lifetime. That fact plus the names tell a lot about me. Let me explain:

Nathaniel Robert Winetzky

I was named Nathaniel Robert Winetzky. It's on my birth certificate. For the first few years of my life that was my actual name. My paternal grandfather fled the Ukraine at the beginning of the 20th century. The Czar of Russia ruled that country and drafted Abraham into his army. On the run he could not use his real name. He was born close to the town of Vinetz; so he used that as his last name as he crossed the frontier into Poland. With money he had saved all his life sewed into his clothing, he was able to buy an exit visa and steerage on a ship leaving Gdansk for Glasgow, Scotland then on to the United States.

At Ellis Island the immigration officer did not think Abraham Vinetz was a good name for someone from Poland. The officer changed the "V" to a" W" added the "KY" at the end. "There, Winetzky," he said," now you sound like a good 'Pollock.'"

When I was quite young, Grandpa Abe took me to the Statue of Liberty. That landmark was the first thing he saw when he entered New York and the United States. To him she represented freedom. He loved that woman almost as much as his lifelong wife.

Nathaniel Robert Winters

When I was three-years-old my mother's side of the family moved to Omaha, Nebraska. My Dad, mother, sister and I followed, a good job was offered to my father as a salesman. He had been involved in the Jewish Mafia during prohibition and then as a union organizer before enlisting in the Navy after Pearl Harbor. My father took a very active role during World War II that included landing troops at D-Day. He wanted a more American name in his new job as a salesman in the conservative mid-western city. He also didn't want anyone from his gangster days to come looking for him.

Nicky Winters

I was seven when my mother died of cancer. I barely remember her. My father heartbroken and desperate moved my older sister and me back to New York City to live with his parents. Unfortunately my Aunt Bonnie started calling me Nicky. I hated Nicky. I wanted to be Bobby, from my middle name. Bobby Richardson was the second basemen for the New York Yankees. I wanted to be like him.

Bobby

By the time my father remarried, everyone called me Bobby, even Aunt Bonnie. The marriage was a total surprise. Two days before my ninth birthday, we moved to Valley Stream, on the South part of Long Island, just outside of New York City. My new family members, an older sister, two younger brothers and my new step-mother joined my sister and father calling me Bobby. It never changed. To my immediate family, a dysfunctional Brady Bunch, I was and will always be Bobby.

Bob "The Stickman"

In high school, Bob replaced Bobby. My friends and I always were giving each other nicknames. My favorite came in high school when I bought my first car, a 57 Chevy with a manual transmission, a three speed, sometimes called a stick shift. So I became "the stickman "like a superhero, Spiderman or Batman. I could have used a super power. Lacking confidence, high school did not come easy for me academically or socially. I played on teams, wrestling, baseball and even football. Not a superstar, I grew into my body on the later side and was a little clumsy until an adult when I became much more successful at athletics even playing college soccer. I remember loving history early, the only subject I received straight 'A' grades. I usually had the textbook read by the second week of school.

Robert N. Winters

I'm not sure when the change became official. I dropped the Nathaniel and became Robert N. Winters. I do know my driver's license and high school yearbook lists me as Robert N. Winters. My Naval records show Robert as my first name also.

Robert N. Winters, U. S. Navy

Vietnam loomed large for my generation. Adolescent rebellion led a major dispute with my parents. My grades were just average and minimum wage jobs would not get me through college. I was not going to wait to be drafted. Like my father did, I enlisted in the Navy just after high school graduation. After three years and a tour in Vietnam my enlistment ended. I came to San Francisco for my discharge, fell in love with Northern California and started college.

Buffalo Bob

I rented a room with my dog Ripple in Oakland, California. Six of us lived in that house, sharing expenses and chores. There were lots of Bobs in the group of people we knew, to differentiate; some friends started calling me Ripple Bob after my dog. That would not do. Gerry, a housemate, was divorced and his children visited on weekends. He took them to a Howdy Doody television show revival with Big Buffalo Bob. The kids started calling me Buffalo Bob. The nickname stuck and I was called Buffalo Bob or just Buffalo throughout my college days in Oakland and at Sonoma State.

Mr. Winters

After college graduation and student teaching at Petaluma High School, I became a full time teacher and coach mostly at Roselawn Continuation (at risk students) High School in Turlock, California. Thirty graduating classes attended Social Studies and Science classes with Mr. Winters. I loved teaching most of the time but it was difficult working with students that often rebelled against their teachers. It took patience. When students got excited about learning it was magic which happened daily. Teaching was easy, discipline and class control was hard. It took constant vigilance and awareness.

I also coached at Turlock High School some freshman baseball but mostly varsity soccer. I started the soccer program at the school finding success with mostly foreign students. As the sport grew in America, I ran soccer summer camps. I passed the torch after ten years leaving the program that I built in good shape. I decided the job of teaching was engaging enough without running off each day to coach.

A career in teaching is like running a marathon not a sprint. No regrets, It was a labor of love. Three unsuccessful back surgeries ended my classroom duties. Chronic pain was so debilitating for two years I was confined to bed rest. I had to retire from teaching. My life improved after attending the Feinberg Pain Clinic. After the clinic felt like I graduated to my next phase of life, not retired.

Nathaniel Robert Winters

I wrote my first book the novella, **Rumors about my Father**, in 2005 as a tribute to my diseased Dad. I always thought that part of teaching history was being a good story teller. Through stories about people, history comes alive. I felt my students might get excited if they could read a story by their teacher and get Twentieth Century history through a character in which they could identify. It was a success in the classroom, the first book many of them had ever read.

That was the start of my work as an author. Three novellas followed: *The Legend of Heath Angelo, Finding Shelter from the Cold,* **and** *No Place for a Wallflower.* At the same time I took classes and conferences about the craft of writing. I met with two critique groups a week, one poetry, the other prose.

It was during this period I noticed a tremor in my left arm. After examination I was diagnosed with Parkinson's disease. Thanks to medication and meditation the effects of the disease remains mild. So I keep writing. As the great Mohammad Ali, who also has Parkinson's, exemplified-If you get knocked down get right back up and keep swinging. In 2013 I completed my first novel, *The Adventures of the Omaha Kid.* My second, *The Penngrove Ponderosa* is to be released in January 2014.

As an author it was time to reclaim the name Nathaniel. It sounds like a writer, like Nathaniel Hawthorne, who said, "Easy reading is damn hard writing." I've learned that lesson. Having Parkinson's disease and dealing with chronic pain gives me a unique voice. I count all my blessings and enjoy every day.

Last week I was in a writing class and there was another Bob. The teacher asked, "Should I call you Bob one and two?

I answered, "You can call me Nate… and so my name and I continue to evolve.

The next poem is dedicated to my in-laws, the Pierce Family.

2. ST PATRICK'S DAY 2012

The rain splashes down, like tears yet unshed.

Edward closes his eyes sees her face.

*

Their Irish fore-families came to the United States

looking for freedom, away from repression,

the memories of starvation during the potato famine.

Settled in the Midwest, the heartland of plenty,

yet even in this new land a depression left them hungry.

Ed and Virginia went to the army

as the world raged at war.

He learned to fly.

She learned to remove a bullet

or hold the hand of a soldier,

crying out for his mother

as the boy was about to die.

They found each other just after that horrific war,

looking for love, finding it together.

The two from "the greatest generation"

created their own special baby boom-

seven children, four boys and three girls.

Survived the bone chilling cold winters of Minnesota,

he bringing home the bacon, she cooking it up.

Politically they were an odd couple

mixed like oil and vinegar.

He was the quiet conservative Republican,

she the soap box Democrat.

Tossed together the two provided their children

a cohesive yet diverse flavor.

The flock of children would gather around their mother

chanting "we all love, we all love."

When all the birds left the nest

so did the eagle and the dove

to the dessert to trade golf balls for the ones made of snow.

*

As the storm rages above the Napa Valley,

the children rally together

from two continents,

indeed "they all love."

For it is St Patrick's Day,

Mentally, Ed must be doing a jig,

thanking the leprechaun,

this family-his pot of gold

Our Twentieth Anniversary:

3. For Colleen, April 11, 2012

April comes and blooms,

such beauty to behold in Northern California,

but my mind wonders back to another April day

with the view of the wind whipped waves of Lake Tahoe.

When two April fools vowed to love, and wed.

You looked so beautiful dressed in white and lace,

I dressed in black and white looked... looked only at you.

The wind howled, like a lonely wolf calling to his mate

and our packs were united, trusting in other fate.

How did twenty years go so fast?

While our little pup grew so big?

The storms of winter have put us to the test.

Yet devotion and commitment stands firm,

like redwood trees on a fern covered hillside.

Spring sun warms the California sky,

the wolf pup will soon leave its winter den to play and hunt.

I renew my vow to be yours to have and hold,

for I love you more than even that Tahoe yesterday.

4. *The Long Hard Trail*

July 22, 2013

Since the Travon Martin trial every pundit on the left and the right are all brilliant experts on prejudice. I know we have come a long way in this country and the world to help people of all backgrounds to get along better. Still discrimination rears its ugly head relentlessly.

Growing up in the shadow of World War II, the concept that a "civilized country" could put 6 to 10 million civilians to death because they were Jews, gypsies or homosexuals is hard to believe. Yet during that war the United States sent Japanese-Americans to relocation camps and confiscated their property. Today secular fighting continues throughout the planet.

I've seen the hostility first hand. People with no idea of my ethnic background tell me they were going to "Jew someone down" and get a better price. As a teacher and growing up in New York I heard all the profane words constantly: kike, nigger, pollok, mick, slant eyes, honkey, white trash, faggot- need I go on? My point is the harshness, cruelty and hostility is not confined to one group of people or a certain race. It lives deep inside all of us. We must fight it every day.

When we see what we are up against it seems so overwhelming. In the face of this, awesome problem, what do we do? I recently read Cheryl Strayed's book *Wild*. She hikes and challenges the grandeur of Pacific Crest Trail. It reminded me of the summer of 1973 when I backpacked in the mountains or the American West with majestic names like The High Sierra, Desolation Wilderness, Olympic Rain Forest, Upper Cascades, etcetera. I can still remember my first climb above Big Sir, into the Ventana Wilderness. I looked at the mountain and my topographical map. Switchbacks climbed four thousand feet straight up. With a fifty pound pack on my back I wondered, like the author in the book, how am I ever going to get over these mountains? We both came to the same conclusion, one step at a time.

5. *Dreams*

November 2012

Dr. Martin Luther King Jr.'s Dream included the notion that

his children could live in a nation and not be judged by the color of

their skin, but the content of their character.

Were the two Obama elections what he saw from the

mountain top?

After Obama's second election, I had my own dream about

race and one's outer pigment.

Autumn, my golden lab said to Coco, my black lab,

"Can you believe that people care so much about the color of

one's coat?"

"No, that's so dumb. Dogs would never do that.

When I smell another dogs butt,

 we all look about the same."

6.   The October Invasion

They came from the southwest first appearing in the
summer of 2010.   Some entomologists believed they were a
mutated desert variety. By October of 2012 the large black
ants infected the whole Midwestern United States. It was
discovered that they lay their eggs in riverbanks, or near
water, and swarm into the cities in the cool of the evening.
They were carnivorous leaving nasty bites to warm blood
animals of the bird and mammal phyla, like some type of
plague of biblical proportions.

The States of Michigan, Ohio and Missouri called out
their best specialists and the militia.   They fought back against
the onslaught. Massive budgets were provided to the local
combatants. Experts studied the insect's mode of operation

extensively on film. The mutant strain of ants were beaten back and appeared to be defeated but like cockroaches they survived all attempts to wipe them out. They came back stronger than ever.

They sweep though the city of Detroit attacking even in the zoo biting so furiously even big cats were left emaciated. Looking closely at the bugs you could see they had bright orange mandibles. Finally the entomologists realized they were not from the desert after all but from Northern California. They had been developed in a laboratory next to San Francisco Bay, combining South American with North American varieties. The ravaged Midwesterners finally realized what type of ant they were up against. They were the World Champion Gi-ants.

I am a life-long Giants fan. In 2012 they won the playoffs and World Series. Did you guess this was about them? So is the next article.

7. The Lands of the Giants

I grew up in a magic land of **Giants,**
it had the tallest buildings in the world.
A lovely giant woman welcomed newcomers,
standing magnificent above the great harbor.

I loved to watch those **Giants** play.

Of course being **Giants** they played ball *uptown,*
in the only place big enough, the *Polo Grounds.*
Their best player had a game so large
He had to reach down to catch a fly ball.

But the people stopped believing in **Giants,**
would not come to watch them play
or build them a giant sized new home.

So the **Giants** moved to a new magic land,
where the hills climb halfway to the stars
and giant trees grow so tall they block out the daytime sun

The people in this new land believed in the **Giants,**
built them a "gigantic" new home.

I climbed the beanstalk and followed the goliaths to the new
land.

I still love to watch the **Giants** play.

Then super storm Sandy hit the Northeast:

8. Ocean Soundtrack Revisited
October 2012

In my adult playground, San Francisco, *there was dancing in the street.*

While back in the land of my youth, Long Beach, NY,

the sounds of silence could be loudly heard

waiting for that *evil woman* named Sandy.

The *eve of destruction* came.

Many a summer day and night

I drove my Chevy past the tidal *levee*

to play with the other *beach boys* and *surfer girls.*

We would do *the swim* thing, or just hang out,

under the boardwalk, on a blanket with my baby.

She was just 17, wearing only a *tiny yellow polka-dot bikini.*

She drove me crazy, like *I was born to be wild.*

When we got hungry we just went

up on the roof of the boardwalk,

got a *cheeseburger in* this *paradise.*

Now it's all gone.

The grand boardwalk was a *wipe out* driftwood

in the ocean or on the beach of this nightmarish *surf city*.

They say they will rebuild, but the globally warming tides are

still rising

And it doesn't take a weatherman

to know which way this wind is blows.

Napa Valley   November 28, 2012

9. *Nature's Requiem*

Gray replaces the golden glow sky of last week.
Stratus hugs the redwood hills above the valley floor,
not the feathery light touch of summer's fog,
but a full embrace of the coming storm's passionate fury.
The shedding leaves surrender their brilliant yellow hue,
suddenly darker colors,
shades of deep purple, and lifeless black,
join last week's turkey, a skeleton, stripped of life and joy.

Seven turkey vultures sit silently atop undressed walnut trees,
birds with scarlet- red plumage on their heads, awaiting blood
like they know Autumn's death is near.
Scavengers devour the fallen, flora and fauna.

Branches reach out, almost naked against the deluge.
Winter's harsh tears clean the air,
wash away our sins, like holy water
'till Spring and life reborn.

10. *Mother Nature's Not So Funny Side*

March 2013

Mother Nature must have a good sense of humor

Watching man mess with her gift of evolution

Noble wolf transitions to barking rat called Chihuahua

Earth mother's smile turns upside down

Watching man mess with her gift of evolution

Polar bears hunt for ice

Earth mother's smile turns upside down

Her world warmer, storms bigger

As the polar bears hunt for ice

Is she still laughing?

Her world warmer, storms bigger

Are those her tears?

Is she still laughing?

At the joke, as her species disappear

Are those her tears?

Mother Nature must have a good sense of humor

It's time for two Halloween type stories:

11. *The Not So Friendly Ghosts*

October 23, 2012

Was it a coincidence that this little escapade took place on Halloween or were the spirits of Alfred Hitchcock and Edger Allen Poe trying to tell me something? The holiday took place on a Saturday that year and I was home with my 5-year–old son. He was watching the movie video, *Casper, the Friendly Ghost.* The costume of the young ghost was waiting in his room for trick or treat. About half way through the cartoon, we heard a tapping on the second floor.

Sam looked at me his eyes opened wide and said, "Dad, did you hear that?"

I smiled and said quite calmly, "I'm sure it is nothing." While I was thinking, what the heck was that? The tapping continued. "I'll check it out. Do you want to go with me?"

"No," he said emphatically.

"Ok, I'll go." Up the stairs I went. I checked all the rooms but could find nothing. While I was on the second floor the sound stopped, but as soon as I descended, there it was again, "Tap, tap, tap."

Four times this scenario repeated. I would go look and the tapping would stop, and then return to my son and it would start again.

Sam stood up, clearly *freaked-out*. "Should we call the police?" He asked seriously.

I laughed. "Maybe we should call ghost busters."

"What's that?" He had not seen the movie yet and was too young to remember the popular group of spirit catchers.

"Never mind," I said. "I'm going outside. Maybe I'll see something." This time he followed me out, like my shadow. Sure enough, outside the second floor front bedroom window was the answer to the mystery. Two crows stood on the landing in front of the window, which faced west and the hot afternoon sunshine, so the glass was coated with a reflective film. The crows seeing their mirror image pecked at their rivals inside the window like a canary attacks a mirror in a birdcage.

I sprayed them with the hose and "Heckle" and "Jeckle" departed, only to return five minutes later.

"Come on Sam." I said as I led him to the car for a quick trip to the hardware store. We need a true Halloween worthy scare crow. Returning, I went up a ladder and placed the wooden owl on the window landing. It worked perfectly. Came the crows, never more.

12. Friday the Fourteenth

Reprinted from *Rumors about my Father and other Stories*

It was not a great day for Wendy Paterson. The nineteen-year old girl had not done well on her economics test at Merritt College. Wendy met with the instructor, Mr. Tanner and creep made a pass at her. She showed her contempt and told him off, and now she was worried about her grade. She was use to guys her age flirting with her, but not her teacher. It had made her very uncomfortable. Wendy had long blond hair, striking blue eyes, and the slim figure of a runner; she was on the track team. Her long legs helped her stride in the distance races.

As she left the classroom building, she looked out at the pouring rain coming down in the Oakland hills, on this ominous January day at four in the late afternoon, darkness rushed towards her. *Damn*, she thought to herself. *This day just keeps getting worse.* She pulled up the hood on her jacket and made a beeline to the parking lot, jogging as her book bag bounced on her back. She was wearing high-heeled shoes and they made it difficult to run on the wet sidewalk. She slipped, broke a heel, and fell headlong into a wet bush. Approaching her car, she found her keys, opened the door and showing her disgust threw her books across to the passenger seat. As the starter cranked over, the car would not kick alive. "Come on, come on, please start," she said out loud to her five year old Honda that her parents had bought her to commute to college. On the third try the engine finally turned over, coming to life. The inside of the windshield was covered with moisture and she blasted the defroster and started the windshield wipers. Putting the car into gear, Wendy fought to see out the windshield as the rain and fog devoured the automobile.

Carefully she turned out of the parking lot and headed for home. Wendy was still living with her family in the suburbs of the Oakland Hills. The house of her childhood was a three bedroom located on a cul-de-sac about ten miles north of the college campus.

Her radio was tuned to KCBS, the San Francisco news station. There had been an attack of a woman near her neighborhood two days earlier and she wanted to hear if there were any details on the radio. There was the sports report and the weather, then some national news. When the local report came on she started paying close attention.

"Sam Harvey is reporting from the Oakland Police Department with the latest news on the attack of a woman Wednesday in the upper Piedmont area. Sam…"

"Joel, the police are reporting that the women was brutally attacked and sexually assaulted. She is in critical condition at Highlands Hospital The name of the women is being withheld. There are no suspects in this heinous crime at this time. The police are asking for anyone with any information to call their hotline at 551-Tips. A five hundred dollar reward has been offered for any information leading to the arrest of the person who committed this crime. This is Sam Harvey reporting from the Oakland Police department."

"Thanks Sam, what was that number again?"
"Joel that's 551-Tips."
Wendy's cell phone rang.
"Hello," she said, her hands free device turned down the
   radio.
"Wendy, it's Mom, did you hear about the assault? Where
   are you?"

"Yah, I was just listening to the radio. It's awful close to home. Kinda scary, I'll be careful though. I just left school and I'm on the way home."

"How was your day?"

"Terrible, Wendy sighed, I'll tell you about it when I get
    home."

"Ok, bye hon, drive safe."

"Bye Mom, see you soon."

It started raining harder and the wind was blowing the wet eucalyptus leaves across the blacktop. The Honda went around a curve and the back tires skidded across the street. Wendy steered into the skid, remembering her driver's education classes. The car straightened, but she stopped the car by the side of the road a minute to catch her breath and to let her heart slow down. As Wendy's foot came off the brake, she stepped on the gas, the car stalled.

"Damn!" She yelled.

She moved the shifter back into park and turned the key. Nothing happened, the battery was dead. Wendy took out her cell phone and hit speed dial to her Mom, no signal! She could not believe her bad luck. *Let's see, she thought, it is*

Friday, but the thirteenth was yesterday. What to do? It was still raining "cats and dogs," and she was still a half-mile from her house. She thought about her broken shoe. *Screw it,* she thought, *I'll leave my stuff in the car and walk home barefoot.* She zipped up her jacket, pulled up her hood and started walking home.

Darkness was almost complete, the rain and fog grabbed at her jacket. She had to lean into the wind. Before she walked two blocks, she was wet, cold, and shivering in the evening's embrace. Wendy turned the corner into her housing complex and walked past Hillside Elementary School, where years earlier she had been a student. Soaked through to her bones, she was only four blocks from home. Out of the corner of her eye she thought she saw a shadow behind a tree by the elementary school. *Was that a person?* She quickened her pace and thought she heard someone behind her. She looked back quickly and only saw fog and rain coming down behind her. *This is my imagination playing a trick on me,* she thought. *I'm cold, wet and tired and just need to get home. Get it together, you have made this trip from school thousands of times.*

Are you paranoid if there is something real to fear? "she wondered. *That crazy rapist is still out there somewhere. Could he be behind her?* She looked back again, *was that a shadow behind her in the fog?* No, she didn't think so. It was strange, her neighbourhood usually was quiet, but now there were no cars at all. She was just two blocks from her house. *I'm ok,* she thought.

Yes, she heard someone behind her. As she looked back, she saw a man duck behind a tree. Wendy started to run. She could now hear footsteps. The person behind her was running! Wendy was a block from her house and had to turn a corner. She slipped on her wet nylon encased feet and fell. Her knee slammed into the sidewalk. Blood from her knee mixed with the water from the rain and ran down her leg. Wendy was back up in an instant and running again. She didn't look back, but could hear the footsteps getting closer. She was at her house! But he was right behind her. Turning toward the shadowy figure, she screamed at the top of her lungs.

Her fifteen-year old younger brother, Phillip, was staring her in the face. "Wow, Wendy that was quite a scream. Did I scare you? Sorry," he said sarcastically, a smile on his face. Wendy looked at him and did not know to hit him or hug him. "You are going to be so sorry!" she said.

Then Phillip's smirky smile disappeared as Wendy hugged her brother and cried on his shoulder.

13. Sunrise Sonata

January 2013

Sunday morning light peeked

around the curtains into the bedroom.

They awoke, cuddled unhurried.

He kissed her neck, again, then, again.

She cooed,

"My, you're amorous this morning."

He answered with another kiss

Married for many years,

arousing with a lively passion,

filled with desire.

Their bodies played the well-known symphony,

and as music reached the climatic crescendo,

Sunday morning church bells rang.

They laughed at the coincidence of timing,

still in love

14. *A Different Night Before Christmas*
December 31, 2012

It is Christmas Eve and the kids are having trouble sleeping thinking about Santa Claus. I'm having trouble sleeping because in the dim glow of the night light, I am looking up from our guest bed in my sister in law's home at a two foot plastic figurine of Jesus nailed on the cross. Let me explain my unrest.

I grew up in a Jewish house hold in suburban New York. My wife grew up in a Irish-Catholic family, one of seven kids, in Minnesota. We met and fell in love in California, that land of cultural homogony. She claims she is a "recovered Catholic" having left the Church behind. I'm more of an agnostic. We deal with our differences well, she is in charge of her spirituality and I deal with my lack of the whole God thing. But during the holiday period, nestled in the bosom of with my in-laws, a little culture clash is inevitable.

Don't get me wrong. I love my in laws. They are a lot of fun, especially when the scotch starts flowing. My sister in law's hospitality is inviting.

My son is fine with the whole holiday thing. He gets to celebrate Christmas and Hanukkah. When he was in second grade they were making holiday cards in class and he raised his hand. The teacher called on him and he asked. "Which one should I make? I'm half Jewish and half Christmas?"

When I was young I had Christmas envy. Not to take anything away from my Hebrew speaking forefathers, but Christmas is so much cooler than the menorah and candles thing.

So here I was trying to deal with this dying martyr of a deity looking down at me. I attempted to put the whole thing in some type of historical perspective. Jesus was Jewish after all. He would have celebrated Hanukkah. He was trapped in a conquered country where his fellow tribesmen were being corrupted by the powerful Romans. He was preaching non-violent protest and demanding religious freedom. So he was like a combination of Gandhi, Martin Luther King Junior, and Thomas Jefferson. I can get down with that. Most historians believe the timing of the holiday in late December is more about the return of the sun (the winter solstice) rather that God's son's actual birthday.

So let's all have some fun with the lights and the tree. Still that guy on the cross is a bit much. Maybe if I just take him down while we are staying in the room. There that's better.

Now how do I deal with the other big guy in the red suit driving the reindeer? I'll have to do that another time because on reflection of my holiday list, I realize I missed getting someone a present. I have to make a quick trip to the mall. Boy, going to that place be a total mess tonight. Next year maybe we can go to some tropical island where everyone is Buddhist.

15. The following is an excerpt from my novella, *The Legend of Heath Angel;* a fictional account of the life of the man who created the first Nature Conservancy Preserve in California.

APRIL 18, 1906

It was still dark when the ground shook and Heath was thrown out of bed. The bricks of the fireplace and chimney of his house tumbled like they were wood toy blocks knocked down by the hands of the fifteen-year-old boy. His wood-framed Victorian two-story house rocked and rolled on its foundation, but stayed upright.

Heath hit his head hard on the floor. He was dizzy and nauseous like a seasick sailor on a ship for the first time. "What happened? Where am I? What day is it?" He stared up at the ceiling as the house rolled in an aftershock. The boy staggered to his feet and felt his way to flip the switch for the new electric light hanging over his bed. Nothing happened in the dark lonely room. He had no understanding that he was trapped in an event that would change California forever.

The boy found the door knob and had to pull hard to open the door that slid open so easily only yesterday.

"Mom!" he yelled at the closed door of the room across the hallway at the top of the stairs.

"I'm here, son!" He heard her unsteady voice yell back.

He barged into her room and was greeted by the silhouette of his night-gowned mother as the first light of dawn filed through the curtain window at the other end of the room. They hugged, grabbed each other's hand tightly and walked unsteadily down the stairs, his mom holding firmly to the banister. They went out the front door.

Dawn was sending light to the small town of Alameda, located on an island jutting out from the east side of San Francisco Bay, just across the estuary in Oakland. Heath realized that he was dressed in a white cotton nightgown and the morning cold snapped him out of his daze. He smelled smoke and saw flames lick out from the roof of a house two blocks to the west. He heard the sound of the new fire truck with its bell clanging. Alameda had both a new fire truck and a horse drawn wagon at the turn of the century.

Finally his mom broke the silence "That was an earthquake wasn't it?"

"I think so. Are you as cold as I am?"

"Yes." She said but stood aimlessly.

Heath ran into the house, grabbed two throw blankets, came back and put one over the shoulders of his mother and pulled on the other like it was a big overcoat. He did not want to go back upstairs yet to get his clothes.

"Mom, do I have to go to school today?"

The woman turned to her son, looked at him intently, and tears welled up in her eyes. She hugged the boy tightly, not wanting to let go. "No, I don't think you need to go to school today. I have a feeling there won't be school today."

Day was breaking, and as the light illuminated the street, Heath could see that people were gathered in the road, many with nightgowns or robes, a dazed look on their faces. Another aftershock hit and Heath threw himself to the ground, hoping to avoid falling. The young man heard more bricks falling and just then noticed the condition of the chimney on his house. Bricks were scattered on the south side of the dwelling and into the street. He noticed that many of his neighbors' brick houses had serious damage.

"Mom, look." Heath said and pointed to the bricks all over the street. The fire from the house two blocks down grew but he could see there were already streams of water being hosed onto the blaze. People were already starting to mobilize, piling bricks out of the middle of the street and in front of houses. "Mom, can I go help?"

The woman looked at him longingly but said "If you must, but I want you to check in with me by lunchtime."

The boy carefully ascended the stairs, threw on a pair of Levis, a flannel shirt, and grabbed a wool sweater. He hurried down the street to the closest fire, while noticing other fires on the island, most of which started when fireplaces had collapsed. Firemen, both volunteer and professional, would be spread thin.

"I'm here to help if you need me," he yelled to the fireman aiming water from a hose. The yellow rain coated man said to the boy, "Kid, grab the back of the hose behind me and keep it steady."

The flames were retreating from the timely attack of water. After about fifteen minutes, a volunteer with a fire helmet came over and relieved Heath on the hose. "I've got it from here." He said.

Heath was then free to wander around the village assessing the damage. He met up with Joe Silva, a friend from school. They noticed that most of the wood houses seemed to have just superficial damage except for the collapsed chimneys. Buildings made of brick were heavily damaged. As the boys were scouting the neighborhood, they noticed an overflowing ferry pulling into the dock. The boat stopped at Alameda on the way to Oakland from San Francisco. The 10:23 arrival was full of passengers carrying luggage, boxes, anything they could carry, leading the beginning of an exodus from earthquake damage in San Francisco to the east bay. Most of the passengers were going on to Oakland, but a few got off the boat at the Alameda mooring, and spread the news of the fire enveloping the city to the west. Hundreds of buildings were heavily damaged and multiple fires were blazing out of control all over the San Francisco Peninsula, whipped by the ocean wind.

The boys ran across the island to the beach on the bay and looked west. They could see the smoke rising from the city. Watercrafts of every type were on the bay. Those with motors mixed with masts leading an escape for a stunned and threatened populous.

By noon, the friends were back at Heath's house where Mrs. Angelo was running an assembly line, making salami sandwiches. "Take one each boys, I'm making the rest for the neighbors whose houses were badly damaged."

"Mom, have you seen all the people coming across the bay from San Francisco? They say the city is a disaster and fires are burning everywhere. We were told that Marshall Law has been declared and the army is shooting looters. I hope dad is okay.

As they were eating at the kitchen table, a powerful aftershock rocked the house sending dishes and china knickknacks to the floor. Mrs. Angelo had just finished sweeping up all the glass from the morning spillage. The stress momentarily overwhelmed her and she sat at the table and cried. Heath got up, put his arms around her shoulders and kissed her on the cheek. He never saw her cry like this, even during the divorce.

"Do you want me to finish the sandwiches?" he asked.

His mother wiped her face in a dishtowel. "No, I'm alright. I'll finish the sandwiches, but I need you to sweep up. Then go out to the street and pile bricks from the chimney. It looks like I'm going to need your help all afternoon. We need to pitch the big camping tent in the backyard. People are going to need places to sleep."

As he finished his chores in the early afternoon, Heath could see smoke starting to hover over the bay mixing with the natural fog. He could smell it coming out of the west. Then he heard an explosion. The army in San Francisco had started using dynamite to build firebreaks. The military's well-intended but futile attack did almost as much damage as the earthquake. The seismic waves had damaged the water mains underground rendering the mostly modern fire department helpless.

Heath watched the setting sun explode in an orange glow in the smoky sky above the bay. Heath thought about his father in San Francisco wondering if he was all right. A chill grabbed him as wind whipped down his shirt. Heath never really worried about his father who seemed amazingly resourceful and self-sufficient, until he heard the first explosion.

His dad had moved to San Francisco after the divorce two years ago. They did not see each other often but the man was still a big part of the boy's life. Now he yearned for his father like he did right after their first separation.

His parents had fought so much in the months before the divorce, what he remembered most about his father's absence was the quiet. His parents were no longer screaming at each other. His mother actually seemed relieved. Yet, as the evening closed in, he realized he missed his dad on this fateful day.

Then out of the glow coming from the dock he saw the familiar figure of his father. For the first time since he had been thrown out of bed that morning, he felt safe.

16. A True War Hero

November 6, 2013

How can a King lose a war and become one of the greatest heroes in World History? It is a story of great bravery a little bit of a myth and circumstance. King Christian X of Denmark was faced with two untenable decisions during World War II and history shows that his decision making leadership was infallible.

After the defeat of France and Belgium by the Germans in 1940 tiny Denmark faced the overwhelming Nazi forces as they invaded the country. After some token resistance, the Danish Government having consulted the King, decided to capitulate rather than put up an impossible defense and tremendous loss of life. Hitler, delighted by the surrender, called his occupation a protectorate and the Germans allowed the Danish Government to continue to rule throughout 1940 to 1942.

The Dictator deported Jews in other occupied countries but knowing that the Danish people supported their Jewish compatriots ignored the "Jewish problem" in Denmark. That policy changed in August of 1943. The Gestapo was ordered to start the evacuation of the Jews in Denmark.

Here is where the myth comes to play. When just before the Jewish New Year, the Jews were ordered to wear the Star of David to make identification easy for the Nazis.

Supposedly King Christian wore the Star and the people of the nation followed his example and totally confused the occupational forces attempting the round up. Is the story true? Weeelll...maybe, maybe not...like George Washington and the cherry tree it's the symbolism that counts.

The Danish King and his people did a Gandhi like resistance. The hid their follow citizens and embarked on a Dunkirk like evacuation of the Jewish people across the water to nearby unoccupied Sweden. Only about five hundred Jews were deported. Over seven thousand escaped right under the noses of the Nazis. This brave defiance probably made life more difficult for the Danish people. Yet they were the only country to make it a national policy to defy the German deportment of Jews.

Few people know about this amazing story today. It should be retold over and over. Hail King Christian X. As Jews say about the holocaust, never forget.

17. Bagels
November 10, 2013

The bagel, the round roll with the round hole
nothing embodies Jewish New York like the bagel,
hard on the outside and soft inside

Few know that a "real" bagel
must be boiled before baked,
ones that aren't like Noah's are faked.

To get bageled means nothing;
To get bagels meant everything, love,
first thing Sunday morning
with the New York Harold Tribune.

A dozen always included an extra,
in case a friend stayed over,
so fresh hot from the oven,
 no need for the toaster.

My favorite was with onion and garlic
with a smear of cream cheese
and strawberry jam,
 but of course never ham.

Dad liked his with lox,
from Nova Scotia; that's Canada.
Grandpa from Poland, like original bagels,
topped the cream cheese with pickled herring.

Dad could get a whole family of smiles,
driving two miles
for a holy bag of bagels,
his heavenly weekly chore.

18. The High Holy Daze Day Dream

God turned to his heavenly counsel of Gandhi, Buddha, Jesus, Mohammad and Moses, a look of disgust occupied his bearded face. "Those religious fanatics are playing God again," he thundered.

"Which ones this time?" Ghandi asked.

"All of them, Moslems, Christians, Hindus and Jews; each think they are the only path to righteousness; claim to know what I want. Then they have to fight each other in wars to satisfy their delusions. Jesus, why didn't they get your message of peace when I sent you there?"

"Lord did you forget that whole Crucifixion thing?"

"Of course not, I just was hoping that they might evolve faster. I worked almost all of day four on that evolution plan." He shook his head in sadness.

"I spent a good deal of time making women as attractive as the flowers in bloom. Yet all the extreme religious zealots want to do is tell those amazing beauties to cover up their bodies. That amount of loveliness is one of my greatest works.

And don't get me started about the nature thing again; it took me almost a whole day of creation, to balance the whole climate thing. Those big brained monkeys screw up my perfect atmosphere in just on century, producing greenhouse gases and cutting down trees. When the resulting climate change causes floods, famine and hurricanes; they have the nerve to call it an act of God. Sometimes I feel like that Jewish comedian."

"Woody Allen?" Gandhi asked.

"No Rodney Dangerfield. 'I get no respect.'"

Moses suggested. "Maybe it's time you want to come down with your wrath."

"No." God sighed. "I've tried that. They never learn. "

"So what are you going to do?" Mohammad asked.

"I think I'll just let them deal with their own Karma."

Writing group assignment: Write a story as the opposite sex.

19. *Another West Side Story*

I had just graduated from Columbia with a degree in English Literature. I was staying in the New York Hilton on west 54th street, having just seen the play *West Side Story* with my parents. It was their graduation present, along with the stay at the hotel. I had one more night before in the big city before I turned back into Cinderella, going home to Albany. My parents left an hour earlier; their car full of things from my dorm room. I was nursing a drink and smoking a cigarette in the bar feeling a little sorry for myself, not having met Prince Charming at college. What does one do with a degree in English Lit? Did I really want to teach nouns and verbs to a bunch of pimply teenagers?

Then if by magic he walked into the bar and sat next to me. "I'll have a scotch neat," He said to the bartender.

Paul Newman was sitting next to me! He was shorter than I expected but the man had to bluest eyes I had ever seen. He turned to me and smiled. I almost melted.

"I don't suppose I could bum one of those from you. I'm trying to quit, but it's hard."

"Sure Mr. Newman." I held out the pack trying to keep my hand from shaking.

"Please call me Paul and let me buy you one of those...what are you drinking?" He nodded to the bartender.

"A Manhattan."

He laughed. "How appropriate."

I couldn't help myself, I gushed. "Mr. Newman, I loved you in *Butch Cassidy and the Sundance Kid*."

"Please call me Paul."

"Yes Mr...Paul, I really did like it. You and Mr. Redford were amazing. Are you friends like that when you're not doing a movie?"

"Friendly enough. He actually is a great guy. But we don't get together very often. We both are on the road making movies. He likes to ski and I like to race cars."

"Are you in town making a movie?" I asked trying to keep his attention.

"No, doing a fund rising event for the Democratic Party." He looked at his watch." I'd like to talk to you some more, you seem very nice, but I've got to run." Paul finished his drink, peeled off a twenty and left it on the bar. He thanked me for the cigarette and stood up.

"Paul, will you sign this for me, no one will believe…"

"Sure, who do I make it out to?"

"Cathy."

He wrote something on my *West Side Story* program, handed it to me and sauntered away like a cowboy in a western movie. I looked at the program.

To Cathy,

Thanks for the smoke, pretty lady

Paul Newman.

I saved that program of *West Side Story. Butch Cassidy and the Sundance Kid* is still one of my favorite movies. Every time I buy salad dressing, I think of the night Paul Newman called me a pretty lady and bought me a drink.

20. Bay City Woman

April 2013

I fell in love at first sight

coming out of the fog into her sunshine,

sailing under her bridge from turbulent waters

her stunning curves, so attractive

as she danced with rock and roll rhythm

my eyes awash in her beauty, my heart aflutter

hooked, at once home

I loved even her manic personality

so high and low, we all have our faults,

tried to understand the shifts

studied her psychology, her geology

rolled with the mood swings

planted my roots deep in her shaky foundation.

21. Saturday Morning Heroes

April 2013

When I was an eight-year-old my heroes appeared like clockwork every Saturday morning on the black and white rabbit eared way back machine. My grandfather and I would be occupied for three hours of Western justice, with lessons to be learned as important as any school, church or temple.

Grandpa Abe, a refugee of Eastern injustice, found sanctuary in the old West. We started with the Cisco Kid, yes there was a Mexican hero on 50's TV, just no Black heroes on the black and white picture tube- but my elementary age mind did not deal gray moral issues yet. Good and evil was much more black and white. The hero always won, the bad guy captured or shot without bleeding and the girl was always saved all in a half hour show complete with Tony the Tiger commercials.

Then came the Lone Ranger with his good Indian partner Tonto, even Indians could be good guys on Saturday mornings. Long before the Beatles, my favorite tune was The William Tell Overture that ended with "High ho Silver, away."

Rin- tin-tin was next, starting my love affair with dogs. Before I ever had a dog, the TV German-Shepard who was a member of the Western U.S. Army, saved the day and showed me the value of having a canine best friend.

We moved to the twentieth century with Roy Rogers who could drive a jeep as well as ride his horse while singing with his wife Dale Evens. He could play a guitar and a six shooter.

The morning ended with a modern day western pilot, Sky King with his lovely often imperiled niece Penny. No worries, she would get into trouble but never was she really in jeopardy. Remember on Saturday morning in the late 50's all the girls were saved, all the bad guys went to jail and all my heroes would ride off into the Western sunset.

I so enjoyed those idealist shows of black and white while eating frosted flakes with my father's Elis Island immigrant father. Reality would come soon enough to take my genuine hero, grandfather to his final sunset.

22.   *Late Night Jitterbug*

A rose in full bloom is so beautiful
ruby lips and cheeks silky smooth
the fragrance intoxicating
no place or time for a wallflower

like the flora in a Disney Cartoon
this special flower moved to music
held the wounded in embrace
a last dance for the dying

She came to me, long wilted
her pollen played into seeds spread
across the countryside
new flowers to behold

She shared with me
the splendid flavor
of her rose hip tea
brewed carefully, a tasty blend

the tea sustained so many

 the pot never went dry

we moved in jazzy rhythm

one last late evening dance

This last poem was inspired by Iola Hitt, a World War II Veteran. She was a spry ninety-two years old in 2012 when I met her. She asked me to write her war story. *No Place for a Wallflower* is the result

23. This is a short excerpt from *No Place for a Wallflower:*

November 15, 1944   La Havre, France

After five days at sea, we arrived at the port of La Havre, France. It was bustling with activity. Soldiers were gathered in trucks and moved out almost a fast as they came in. Supplies were unloaded from the cargo ships with never ending lines of army workers. Then another group would reload them onto convoys of trucks. It reminded me of ants on the farm.

Many buildings had been extensively damaged. The ruble had been moved out of the streets but sat piled high by the sides of the road. Both, the Allies and Germans rained bombs down on this important port. It would take years to make this city whole again.

I was called aside by my CO, Major Pam Jenkins. "You wanted to see me ma'am," I said.
"Sit down, Lieutenant," she said with a frown on her face. "I wish there was a better time and place to give you this."

She handed me a letter sized piece of paper. It is a telegram from Mr. and Mrs. Palmer. The paper read: "Iola Bob was shot down over the South Pacific in his B29 and is missing in action. STOP If we hear anything more we will telegram. STOP" Western Union charged by the word. It was so short, so simple and so heartbreaking. The telegram was dated October 2. It had taken that long to catch up with me. I never did meet Bob's parents. In some ways, being in the army when you got this kind of news was hard, you could never alone. I went to my bunk and cried. Work quickly spread around the unit. In other ways, being in the army when you go this type of news was easier because you had to be alone.

After the war, I thought about him sometimes. I loved him. I guess what happened was fate. After all I had a wonderful marriage. But every once in a while I wondered...?

24. *Ode to a Veteran*

November 11, 2012 and reworked November 11, 2013

No big deal, look evil in the face
just save the human race
keep the black storm from our shore
Nothing more

When it was over
never marched in a parade
wanted a medal
just returned to his life,
find himself a wife

Can't let Veteran's day can come and go
remember how much we owe

He drove a landing-craft at Casablanca
then the deadly Norman beach,
front-gate opened, eyes did see
thousands fall on shore, or in blood-red sea
fished them from waves
screaming for bandages or early graves

His little escort joined
a convoy of hope
to bombed out Britain under the gun
and Russia, almost completely over-run

Came they did across the cold Atlantic,
and frozen North Sea, no time to dwell
chased by unseen Wolf-packs from depths of hell
scores of vultures diving from the sky
spitting hot breath of fire, causing thousands to die

If tossed to the water cold death quickly struck
the seas frigid fingers made rescue pure luck

The plucky Convoy fought back
firing clouds full of shot, they called "ack-ack"
so many vultures he could not miss
many ugly birds fell in a burning hiss

His little ship and others chased
Wolf-packs from the seas
depth charged, the U-boats 'till
desperate, alone-brought to their knees

So let us pause, raise a glass, fly the flag,
gather their planted sweet fruit
I remember your nightmares, Dad
Let us toast and salute.

Boatswain's Mate First class Leo Winters 1914-1999

You can read more about Leo in the Novella/Memoir:

Rumors About My Father

I am a Vietnam Veteran. The following story was inspired by my fellow Vets who gave so much

25. *The Round Trip*

Reprinted from *Rumors about my Father and other Stories*

Joe Buckman kissed Lisa and held her in a long embrace. He felt her body next to his and he did not want to let go, like he was taking a mental picture of the feeling. He didn't know when or if he would ever kiss her again.

They had met two weeks earlier in San Francisco, at a Grateful Dead Concert. He had two weeks leave after completing school to be a Personnelman in the Navy. He was 19, the average age of the young men who were dying in Vietnam. She was 18, a senior at Berkeley High School. Since they had met at the beginning of August, they had been together every day. She had long blond hair, wore love beads, and bellbottom pants, the uniform of the anti-war movement in 1970. He also wore bellbottoms, the uniform of the United States Navy.

Lisa gave him a ride to Travis Air force Base to catch a plane. His orders told him to report to the USS Gulf Stream, ARS 53, a rescue salvage ship, which was presently located in DaNang Harbor, Vietnam. They listened to rock and roll on the radio in her Volkswagen Bug, when the music was interrupted by a speech from President Richard Nixon. "Let me make one thing perfectly clear, the war in Vietnam is winding down. I have a secret plan to end the war."

"If that's true, what the hell am I going for?" Petty Officer Buckman asked.

"I could keep driving and take you to Canada."

"No, this is something I've got to do."

He felt very confused. He had been in the Navy for just over a year, enlisting just out of high school. At first, he was proud to wear the uniform, but the more he thought about the war in Vietnam, the more he realized he didn't want to go. As

Mohammad Ali said, "I've got nothing against these Vietnamese." Now they were at the front gate of the Air Force Base. He kissed her again.

"I can't wait to see you when I come back.

"I'd like that, sailor man."

Finally he let her go, turned and walked to the guardhouse at the front gate. He looked back at her. She held up two fingers. "Peace," she yelled at him. He saluted the guard, showed his orders and was directed to the chartered aircraft sitting on the runway. The next stop would be Clark Air force base in the Philippines, then on to Da Nang.

*

Joe Buckman descended the stairs of the Air Force transport. The heat and humidity hit him like an Ali left hook. Within minutes sweat was coming through his dress white uniform. He walked into the terminal and showed the information officer his orders. He was told to have a seat and someone would be with him shortly. Oh yes, he thought, the old military hurry up and wait. He took a seat, and in spite of the fact that it was 10 in the morning, lack of sleep and major jet lag allowed him to doze off in the chair.

"Are you Buckman?"

Joe looked up to see a black Navy petty officer staring down at him.

"Ah, yeah," he said groggily, trying to focus his eyes. "How long..." He looked at his watch. It was 1300.

"I'm Johnson. I've come to take you to the ship."

"Ok, thanks, let me get my sea bag."

"I've got a jeep out front," Johnson said.

They moved out of the terminal and Johnson loaded the sea bag into the back of the jeep.

"I am very glad to see you," Johnson said. "You are my ticket out. Personnelman Buckman, the Gulf Stream is all yours, I'm going home tomorrow. You're my replacement. I'll show you some of your duties here, need to get the ship's mail at the Navy base."

"What's the ship like?" Buckman asked.

"It's an old rust bucket, built for World War II. It's slow and small. One 40mm gun is the only defense, and if we have to use it, we are in real trouble. Half of the 80 man crew are divers, we do rescue and salvage work. The captain is an old enlisted man who worked himself up to Lieutenant Commander the hard way, does everything by the book. The ex-o is your boss. He is a hard-ass Lieutenant, just a year out of Annapolis. And Ortiz, the first class gunner's mate, is a first class jerk, watch out for him. Hey, do you get high?"

"Yea, of course I was at a Dead concert last week. Everyone I know our age smokes weed."

Johnson produced a joint and smiled. "The guys on the ship will want you to get some when you get the mail. You can buy it made to appear to look like cigarette cartons, tax stamped and everything.

"Aren't you worried about getting caught?" Buckman asked.

"Don't worry, I know where to go and I'm careful."

The two drove down an alley and took a smoke break. Then they went back to the Navy base and did the mail run. Finally they drove the jeep back to the ship.

Buckman looked at the Gulf Stream, he was assigned to this ship for the next year. It was small, an oversize tugboat. He boarded the ship carrying his sea bag over his shoulder. He saluted the duty petty officer.

"Permission to come aboard, sir," he said, showing his orders.

"Permission granted."

And just like that, Buckman was a member of the crew.

Johnson took Buckman to see the Executive Officer, Lt. Schulman, and down to his quarters to stow his gear. He was given one small locker and a bunk second from the top. The bunks were stretched canvas, stacked four high. Next to the four "racks," as they were called, was a post and then four more racks. Quarters were very cramped. What could not fit in your two foot by two foot locker, you kept in your sea bag, to be placed in the forward hold. Then Johnson took Buckman to the small office, consisting of two desks, one for yeoman, Tim Larson, and one for him. A Royal manual typewriter was locked down to the desk. Everything had to be locked down, for times of rough seas. Buckman noticed that he was not seasick, but feeling woozy and the ship was still tied to the peer. It was his first sea duty. He wondered how he would feel when the ship gets underway.

The next day, Buckman said goodbye to Johnson.

"Good luck," Buckman said.

"You're the one who needs luck, man, I'm going home," Johnson replied, and laughed.

Joe watched as Johnson saluted the duty officer, the flag on the fantail, and walked off the ship. It was his job now ready or not.

"All hands to special sea detail stations." The order came from the bridge. Buckman made his way to the bridge. He would only watch today, learning his job, a captain's phone talker during sea detail and general quarter's station.

The ship was headed to the DMZ near the border with North Vietnam. An oil tanker had hit a mine and put itself aground to avoid sinking. It was the Gulf Stream's job to use its divers to patch the ship and tow it back to sea. At all ahead standard, the ship made ten knots. It would take all day to get to station.

The sun was setting when the grounded tanker came into view. Buckman looked at the wounded ship on the beach. Oil was leaking into the water and onto a beautiful, clear, coral reef. The jungle came right down to the beach. He thought that this would be the perfect vacation spot if it weren't for this nasty little war. The Gulf Stream dropped anchor and posted guard fore and aft. They would wait until morning to start the arduous task of getting the tanker seaworthy.

In the morning the Gulf Stream moved in close to shore. The workboat was launched, filled with divers to work patching the hole in the oil tanker. Not being a diver, Buckman was given the job of securing a perimeter around the tanker. Ten men from the Gulf Stream were given old M-1 rifles and joined ten members of the tanker crew on guard duty ashore around the workstation. Six divers put on their gear and started working on the patch.

Without warning all hell broke loose. Mortar shells rained down from the sky. The sailors on the beach opened fire with their rifles, but were firing blindly into the jungle. A shell hit the tanker and a fire broke out. From the Gulf Stream's bridge a call for help went out to the fleet. Fifty miles away, two A-4 Phantoms took off from an aircraft carrier and headed to the rescue like John Wayne and the cavalry in a Western Movie. But Vietnam was not Hollywood. A mortar fell close to Buckman. Both his legs felt like they were on fire. He looked down and blood was covering his legs.

"Help, someone help!" he yelled.

The ship's corpsmen ran to his side. He put a tourniquet on each leg. Just then they could hear the jets and the jungle exploded in napalm fire from bombs dropped by the Navy aircraft.

Other sailors appeared with a stretcher and they removed the wounded petty officer from the beach and placed him in the workboat. He passed out.

Buckman awoke with his head in a fog. He was in a helicopter, a morphine drip in his arm. He could not even feel his legs. Were they ok? He didn't know. He stayed in a fog for days, not sure where he was or where he was going. Did he awake on an aircraft? He wasn't sure.

It was a full ten days later that he awoke with consciousness. He was in a hospital. His eyes came into focus. He could see a morphine drip next to his bed attached to his arm. He felt for his legs, they were gone. Tears streamed from his eye and depression hit him hard. He learned he was at the naval hospital in Oakland, California. Doctors came in to talk to him. He would be fitted with artificial legs.

He thought about Lisa, so close, over in Berkeley. He didn't want her to see him like this. He didn't call. His parents came to see him all the way from Pennsylvania. They were happy to see their son, glad he was alive, but he could see the sadness in their faces. They stayed for a week and then headed home. When they left, he felt empty, alone.

In December, Joe Buckman left the hospital for the first time alone. He was in a wheel chair. He took a taxi into San Francisco and told the cabby to drive him around town. He had three months back pay in his pocket; he could afford the cab fare. Over Nob Hill the taxi went, as he watched the tourists board the cable car, something he could not do. Then it was past China Town to North Beach.

"Take me to Sausalito," he said.

The cab turned, headed for the Golden Gate Bridge. Joe thought of Lisa and how he would never see her again. As they got to the bridge, Buckman said to the cab driver, "I've changed my mind. Let me out here."

"Are you sure, here?"

"Yah, help me get the wheel chair out." After he was safely in the chair, he gave the driver a $100 bill. "Thanks, keep the change."

He wheeled the chair onto the bridge with the walkers and bike riders and set out crossing the landmark. The cold wind slapped his face and fog fought against the last bit of sunshine over the Pacific. A purple and red glow appeared on the horizon. Waves crashed below the bridge. Even in the cold air Buckman broke into a sweat from the work of moving his wheel chair along the walkway. As he neared the middle of the bridge, he stopped and looked longingly back at the city he loved. He pulled himself out of his chair and to the side by the cables and dropped over the railing, falling down to the bay. Joe Buckman's name does not appear on the Vietnam Memorial. His death was a suicide. But he died in Vietnam, like the innocence of a generation.

Headline from Sunday's September 2012 San Francisco Chronicle: "2012 WAS THE WARMEST SUMMER IN THE WORLD'S HISTORY."

26. Of Ostriches and Dodo Birds

Iola Hitt, a woman veteran friend called World War II: *No Place for a Wallflower.*

Then the struggle against Global Warming should be: *No Place for an Ostrich*es as humanity stands with heads in the sand, doing nothing and hoping against hope: "that God willin' the creek won't rise." Katrina in New Orleans should have been natures' Pearl Harbor; but no one heeds this call. Soon the grizzly bear and Arctic wolf will go the way of the dinosaur and the Dodo bird. The underwater sand will not provide a refuge to our hidden bird brain Ostrich imitating heads

27. *Not Quite a Love Story*

February 2023

Taking on the job Turlock High School's first soccer coach did not come with the pressures of basketball and football. Unlike the two major high school sports, no one cared about soccer. It would still be a few years before almost every suburban kid played soccer. Back in the 80's soccer in the Central Valley was a winter sport. Forget cheerleaders, even brave parents did not venture out into the thick valley fog to root for their progeny. Why would the masses care about the mostly "English as a second language" crowd? The majority of players were the sons of Assyrians, Portuguese from the Azores, and Mexicans. If I was real lucky a foreign exchange student would show up from England, Brazil, Germany or some other soccer powerhouse where the game was called football.

Without anyone at the school noticing, in 1982 we had a very good team. Jon Shoebridge appeared with the English name and an Argentine Spanish accent to lead the team in scoring. Ramon Garcia showed brilliant footwork to control the midfield. Bellose Lellaham, the captain, had the speed and the smarts to be a great sweeper on defense. We went to the annual early December Fresno tournament in first place with 6-1 record. Still I knew we could be better, the strong individual play had not quite jelled with team proficiency.

It was not a surprise when no adult chaperones volunteered to accompany the team with the coach, just standard procedure. No school bus or funds were allocated from the district. We sold candy bars to help pay for the inexpensive motel.

We won our two games on Saturday putting the team into the semi-finals on Sunday morning. After a gourmet dinner at Round Table and a trip to the market to load the student's down with enough snacks to feed a small country, we withdrew to the motel. Downtown Fresno, even in the 80's, was not the best neighborhood so the rules for the team were clear. Watch television or do something totally unique like read, but stay in your room and lock the door with the deadbolt. Don't open the door for anyone except the coach.

I reminded them, "I will do unexpected bed checks. If anything unusual happens, call me I'm right next door."

About 10pm, my high school teacher intuition came alive like Spiderman's tingly sense. It was too quiet in the next room. I went to investigate, knocking loudly and said," It's Coach Winters let me in." George Agnos came to the door. He looked at me through the gap with the chain lock still on the door. "High coach, we're okay in here."

No, you're not, I thought, "unlock the chain." I heard feet scurrying inside the room.

When George opened the lock I walked right past the beds and into the bathroom. Sure enough two girls hid behind the shower curtain. As I pulled the curtain back one girl smiled shyly, showing a mouth full of braces winding along her teeth. The other taller, more mature looking girl, just shrugged her shoulders.

"Okay girls out." I pretended to be very angry. I read the team the "riot act." "Where in the world did you find them?" I asked George.

"They were in the market when we got snacks. I told them my room number."

"We have an early game, lights out." I gave my best, I'm so disgusted look, and shook my head as I left, secretly impressed with his initiative.

At 11:30 I did final room checks. About midnight I feel asleep. Suddenly I was awakened by a knock on the door. The clock signaled 1:05. "One minute." I yelled and threw on a robe. Unlocking the door I opened it to see two scantily dressed, obvious prostitutes in front of me. "We heard that you are interested in getting lucky," one of them said, smoke billowing at me from her cigarette.

I couldn't help myself. I broke out laughing. "No thanks ladies." I retreated and locked the door.

At breakfast, I didn't say anything about my visitors, to the team. I could see the curious looks on their faces during the meal. I put my game face on, but was laughing on the inside at the thought that they were dying to know how I reacted to the ladies of the night.

We won both games that Sunday, to win the tournament trophy. Ramon admitted to me he scored the winning goal with his hand, a foul, the referee couldn't see in the thick fog. But no one admitted to sending those two women to my room that night.

We won the league that year. I think all the players from different cultures came together as a unit after that weekend in Fresno. Passes became pin-point, positioning became second nature, and everything came together. It was my favorite year as a coach. Maybe I fell a little bit in love with that team.

End

Not Quite a Love Story is mostly factual.

This true story that inspired a chapter in the novel:

The Adventures of the Omaha Kid, which of course is fiction.

28. My step-brother Fred and his two teen age children came to visit last summer. It had been a few years since we had seen each other. He lived in New York and me in California.

That same summer I went back to New York for a visit and stayed at his home in Harlem. We went to a Yankee Game together with our sons. We had a good time catching up. After I returned home I learned he had been hospitalized. He appeared to be healthy when we were together. You never know…

Brothers   *Part I*

We became brothers I-9, he-8,
my father- His mother united us.
Who the hell are you? We both thought,.
our fur ruffled- strange male dogs circling, sniffing.
soon part of a pack, bonded together through life.

Complicated, confusing-siblings
so different-then distant
enemies and allies
foe and friend
hate and love

Some invisible rope tied us together,
frazzled, frayed, strained and stretched-
held together by just a thread, or a phone wire

He lay critical-unconscious, brain bleeding
those strings that bind us are tugging at my heart

July 10, 2013

Brothers   *Part II*

That thin tread finally falls, gentle tug- no more
 I feel his absence slight sad shift of universal weight.

Picture a different time
when we still believed in Camelot
after dinner brothers
playing street football .

That night we were a team, he and I
In front of our house,
those suburban green acres

Fred ran an up and out
just behind our Ford, in front of the Chevy
I threw the perfect pass

He reached out
ball spiraling to his hands
but his image faded-
ball falling, tumbling incomplete.

August 13, 2013

Brothers   Part III

Cloudy the gray morning matches my mood
but by noon eternal Napa sunshine mocks me
smiling face scornful of my tears.

Fred is dead!

Even rhyme ridicules, insulting my pain-
like a slap in the face.

Come Thor bring lightning thunder rain
drive me inside,
let me bow my head and mourn.

Watch the cande bun down
sputter a sparkle as his last light goes out..

Tomorrow the sun can smile again
I'll go to the forest, plant a tree,
watch new life take hold.

But wait please wait 'till tomorrow
let me hold on to the pain
just one more day.

August 20, 2013

Fred Winters 1951-2013

29. Hitting the road
October 2013

Go West young man. Rollin',rollin', keep those doggies rollin, On the Road, or as Mick Jagger sang: *"You got to move, you got to move child, got to move..."*

I tried to count all the times I've moved in my life and believe the figure is 22. Considering I spent 20 years in one house in Modesto, that's a lot of changes of addresses for the Post Office. Sometimes it seems like I've been playing musical chairs with life. In my younger days B.C.-(before Colleen), I never wanted more possessions then I could fit in a pickup truck. I would borrow a friend's wheels, load up and "bam" I was ready to roll.

Many European countries families will stay in the same place for generations. So why do Americans move so often? Maybe it's in our blood. After all, almost all of our forefathers and foremothers came to America from somewhere else.

You may have heard I'm moving again, this time just across town. Does it get easier after all this practice? Hell no!

I would write more on this topic but I've got to move.

31. Excerpt from: *The Adventures of the Omaha Kid:*

Chapter 8
Adirondack Summer Camp
Lake George, New York
Summer 1968

Rhonda Pastrovinsky's body was changing. She was reaching puberty, developing curves, going from an awkward tomboy to a pretty young woman. The Polish-American girl, who was always teased and treated badly by the popular girls at junior high, was now attractive. Boys began to look at her differently and she liked the attention. Here at camp, all the other girls wanted to be her friend.

Carol Simon, her bunk mate, said, "I think Tim Corelli's cute. Don't you?"

"I haven't noticed." Rhonda said as she brushed her sandy brown hair. In fact, Rhonda had noticed him looking at her, and when she looked at him, he would quickly turn away. They had played this game a lot in the last few weeks, him trying to act like he wasn't looking at her.

"He won the camp tennis tournament and is so cute. I think he likes you," Carol stated.

"What makes you think so?"

"Gloria said that Roger told her that Tim told him he likes you."

Rhonda shrugged her shoulders. "Oh well, there's just two weeks of camp left. So what if he likes me." Rhonda did like him but had no clue how to react to this news.

The Adirondack Summer Camp was located in upstate New York near the Vermont border. It was a summer haven for mostly suburban New York and New Jersey adolescents. The beautiful setting in the forested mountains by a large lake became the boys' and girls' natural playground. They could swim, canoe, play games and do all types of arts and crafts. Some could even plot their first romances. Large cabins provided dorms for the kids. Same-aged girls were placed in the same cabin. Boys were grouped the same way on the other side of the mess hall.

The next day Rhonda decided to confront Tim. After breakfast she noticed him glancing over and walked up to him and said, "Hey Timmy, what's the deal? Why are you looking at me?"

"What do you mean?" he said, trying to be cool.

"Meet me in the trees behind the canoe dock in one hour."

"But I'm supposed to play tennis," Tim replied, as he noticed his palms sweating and his heart starting to race.

"I've heard love is supposed to mean nothing in tennis," she said with a laugh, surprising herself with her wit. She walked away and could feel her confidence growing. Tim watched her go, his mouth falling open.

*

Fourteen-year-old Tim was very comfortable on a ball field or a tennis court, but he didn't know how to deal with a pretty girl, especially *this* girl that he had spent the whole summer trying not to have her notice him sneaking glances.

He walked down the path into the forest above the canoe dock. The birch trees were in full maturity, white bark with green leaves hanging in bunches. Bees moved throughout the fertile flowers sucking the sweet nectar, summer in full bloom. He came upon the object of his obsession, Rhonda, who he noticed was wearing pink shorts, her long legs ending in white tennis shoes. Her light blue tee shirt matched her eyes. His mouth went dry.

"Hi Tim," she said with a smile on her face.

"Hi Rhonda. Why did you want me to meet you?" He heard himself saying.

"Someone said that you like me."

"I… maybe… yeah… I mean I think I might." He felt her staring right through him.

"Do you want to kiss me?"

"Sure."

Tim closed his eyes and leaned forward. Rhonda stepped forward and kissed him lightly on the lips. He could feel the hair on the back of his neck standing up. Tim would always remember that first kiss fondly.

"What are you thinking?" Rhonda asked the boy.

"I'm not sure. Maybe we should try that again."

They kissed again, trying too hard, pressing too hard. Their lips just stuck together. "How is that?" Timmy asked.

"Maybe one more time, this time softer."

Their heads moved together slowly, lips joining softly, kissing and then kissing more. "I think we got it right that time." The nervous girl said giggling.

In the next two weeks, they would sneak off and kiss. It was puppy love. Timmy felt so wonderful, so horrible and so unsatisfied.

When camp ended, their parents showed up to take them home. They could not even kiss goodbye. As they drove south in separate cars, going their separate ways, Rhonda cried and Tim smiled.

Praise for *The Adventures of the Omaha Kid:*

The Adventures of the Omaha Kid (Paperback) Colin Alkars

I was initially attracted to this book for its sports themes, but this novel is much more than the story of a remarkable athlete. "The Adventures of the Omaha Kid" engagingly explores themes of identity and relationship - how we go about defining ourselves and finding our place in the world. Winters is a gifted storyteller. His narrative is inventive and his characters are drawn with confidence and care. You'll enjoy your encounter with "The Omaha Kid"

Bob has created something really special…with complex characters…I couldn't put it down. .**Dorothy Mackay** Collins Former curator, Robert Lewis Stevenson Museum

Bob has a great story telling ability. **Ken Klein** author of Thailand Stories

32. This poem *Dark Blues behind the Looking Glass* was written by a character at a pain clinic in *The Adventures of the Omaha Kid*. I think it is powerful but depressing.

Dark Blues behind the Looking Glass

The sun refused to shine
Dark clouds follow me around
Pain racks my body
Gravity is pulling me to the ground.

I'm falling down the rabbit hole
Spinning to a place so bad
Nobody wants to follow
Not even the hatter so mad.

I ask Alice for some of her pills
Hoping to keep my head
But my depression continues
So I refuse to get out of bed.

Here even the Cheshire cat
Refused to send me a smile

The deck of cards shuffle by

I have fallen another mile.

The Queen of Hearts-

trumped by the evil black King.

Will the sun ever shine again?

Will it ever be spring?

33 .Excerpt from: ***Finding Shelter from the Cold,*** a novel for young adults and all who love dogs:

An Ice Age Tale of Wolves and Man

Prologue

The wolf glided quickly across the field. She had picked out her prey, a large deer with huge antlers. The pack looked to her for guidance. She was the alpha-bitch, second in command. The buck was in rut and had just lost a battle to another male for sexual dominance.

It was cold, Ice Age cold, and the wolf had a thick coat of winter white fur. Frozen tundra met the forest. The deer's head bobbed up and down as his antlers scraped against the frozen tree bark. Foam dripped from the buck's mouth and steam rose from his nostrils. He was powerful but exhausted in defeat, vulnerable.

The wolf started the attack, chasing the reindeer. Yet even in exhaustion the deer was quick. Seeing his growling attacker, he bounded off, outracing the sprinting wolf. The prey ran for the open space away from the trees, putting fifty yards between himself and his attacker.

The buck relaxed, feeling safe when the next wolf jumped out. A male leader of the pack had been hiding in plain sight, lying flat against the icy tundra. These canine hunters chased their prey as a pack, in tandem, taking turns to exhaust the deer.

There were five in the pack, a male with a black spot on his muzzle and four females, including the alpha-bitch with a brown spot on her tail. Mostly the wolves were all snowy white.

They exhausted the vanquished buck and he turned to face his attackers. The full pack surrounded their prey. The buck still formidable, his antlers and head bent low ready to charge, but out of breath. The wolves took turns attacking his hind hamstrings. Helpless, the poor creature turned in circles trying to fend them off, his very life at stake. All five canines bore into him, biting at his legs, his throat, tearing the deer's flesh with powerful jaws and sharp teeth.

Soon the wolves' coats were bathed in blood and no longer white. Covered in red, they ripped into chunks of meat. The pack won this Ice Age battle of life and death but things can change quickly. Halfway finished with their meal, twilight descended, sending a glow into the western sky.

A loud roar stopped them in mid-bite. The wolves looked up to see the two huge white arctic lions approaching. The large cats wanted the kill. As formidable as a pack of wolves could be, they were no match for the lions. The male wolf growled, teeth flashing. He tried to defend the carcass, not giving ground fast enough. The first large lion swiped with deadly claws, catching the lone wolf along his right side, leaving a huge gash. The wolf's blood mixed with the deer's on his coat and he retreated, mortally wounded. As the sky darkened and night descended, the young wolf lay dying.

Chapter 1

The Wolf's Story

I held my tail high because I'm the alpha-bitch, proud. I have earned my position by guile, guts and glory. The other female wolves do not have what it takes to be leader. I plan the hunts, find shelter and lead the pack. The male is the absolute leader, but I do most of the real work.

Now the pack looked to me since our leader was down. How stupid to challenge a lion, though males tended to be that way, not knowing when to retreat, when to give up the fight. He lay dying in the snow, whimpering, my lover, my friend, our leader. Six eyes looked at me to lead them.

What to do? I nuzzled my fallen mate. He groaned. I licked his face and turned. With a nod to the rest of the pack, we left. A wounded wolf brings all types of predators.

Temperatures were falling. I could smell snow in the air, and we needed shelter from the storm. We headed to a small cave that we had dug under a rock last summer in the cool mud. It was a few miles away and it was time to go home. We jogged to the cave, our bellies half full but our hearts empty. We crawled under our rock and lay tightly together to share our body heat against the wicked night's cold. Exhausted, we fell into a restless sleep, knowing our pack must change.

The morning dawned colder and wetter. Snow had fallen during the night and crunched under my paws. I liked to walk alone at times, to get away from the others and think.

As clouds hung in the sky I walked to the ridge top to watch the two-legged wolves. They didn't have fur, but wore skin from animals on their backs. They lived in huts during the summer on the ice. I could see the wood and stretched hide that made their shelters.

I called them two-legged wolves because they were smart like us. Like wolves they hunt in packs, taking turns chasing their prey or laying in ambush like we would. But on their paws they had these long digits. They held tools to hunt; long sticks with points or weighted sticks with stones. They needed these tools because they couldn't run fast and their teeth were pathetic.

Gray Ears, another wolf, followed my scent to the ridge. She was the smallest of the pack so her tail was always down between her hind legs. She came to me and rolled on her back offering her belly in submission. I licked her on the mouth in greeting.

Gray Ears rose up with a look on her face that asked "What are you doing?"

I nodded toward the human huts. She shrugged her shoulders. She didn't understand my fascination with the humans but, somehow, I knew humans and wolves were linked.

Praise for *Finding Shelter from the Cold:*

"It reminds me of Jack London, a great adventure for young adults and dog lovers."

Jenny Pessereau, Author

"It is the best book I ever read." Kathy Larson, Seventh Grade Student, Salida Middle School

The following is a Poem about the book:

34 Still Finding Shelter from the Cold

White wolf glides quietly,

stalking her prey

in prehistoric icy wonderland

the buck locked in sight

she springs, diving across the tundra

reindeer flees, eyes escape, evergreens ahead

the pack waits

white- white invisible silent

six pack-mates strike

 powerful jaws take hold,

 tight knife-like

 teeth rip, tear,

red flows on white

seven hungry carnivores

consume chunks of meat

leaving little for scavengers

pack prances away,

bellies full

their distant descendants

will spring,

diving into the SUV

 going home with you and me.

35. This short story, Wind and Rain was previously published in *Rumors about my Father and other stories*.

Wind and Rain
October, 1415

The river moved quickly downstream, fed all day by the heavy rain. Wind whipped its way through the canyon, blowing sheets of water over all in its way. A tall black oak stood on the left bank of the river. It had endured many a cold winter. The old oak was asleep now, naked branches reaching out in the storm.

A squirrel deep inside the tree's body gnawed on an acorn that the tree had been so nice to have left during the autumn. If the squirrel had looked, he would have seen something moving in the distance. A man was riding a black and white horse. The horse's nostrils flared as it tried to breathe in the thick, humid, cold air. Steam rose upward as the animal let his breath out.

The man on the horse had his eyes closed. Sleep tried to overtake him. A coat of steel covered his whole body. A long lance was lashed to the other side of his leather saddle. A shield was lashed to the other side of his heavily burdened horse. Two arrows struck out from the silver fox that stood as his symbol on his shield,

If I don't find shelter soon, he thought, I shall fall to the muddy earth and meet my savior, who through his mercy has spared me in battle. His long brown hair came down to his shoulders, sliding down below his grey helmet. The armed man's groggy brown eyes showed his fatigue when he could shake them open, but his youth showed in his fatigued face. His whole body seemed numb from the cold. Yet on he pushed, hoping against hope to find a village and shelter soon.

Night attacked the daylight in the diurnal battle that the darkness always won. The sky turned a darker shade of grey in the transition. The undressed trees reached out hostilely at the twilight sky. Clouds blocked the rising moon and stars. The man almost fell from his mount due to the cold and fatigue that had driven dizzily into his brain. Catching himself, he opened his bloodshot eyes to see a light in the distance.

Focusing his eyes, he made out a building a mile or so in the direction he was riding. Overjoyed, he spurred his mount to a trot, arriving at this destination minutes later.

As the young knight dismounted, he noticed the light go out between the cracks of the door. The building was an inn, made of wood and standing shabbily, in need of repair. A small stable stood in the back. He knocked on the door, only to be answered by silence. Again he knocked.

"Is anyone there?" he yelled, still greeted with no answer.

"Open or I shall break the door down!" he shouted angrily.

"Please go away," a women's voice begged from behind the closed door.

Surprised by the reply, the soldier mellowed, "Please, I am cold, tired, and hungry. Surely a good Christian cannot refuse one as such."

"But you are dressed for war," the woman replied, fright in her voice.

"I mean no harm, and I can pay for my keep," the knight assured her.

The door opened slowly and a young woman stood in front of the solider. His heart almost stopped and his mouth dropped open at the sight of her. He thought he must have fallen in the mud and was dying, for in front of him stood an angel. Her long golden hair fell down to her slim waist. She wore a simple dress tied in the middle and her bare feet looked cold and pale at the bottom. Her blue eyes showed fright, turning away from his gaze. The man stood speechless.

"Well come in," she said softly," or we will all die from the cold."

A fire was blazing in its place by the side wall. A young boy sat by it. He too had golden hair and the knight assumed he was the young woman's brother. "I would like very much to be out of my armor," the knight said.

The boy and maiden succeeded in helping the young man out of his heavy garments.

The young woman offered him a meal of acorn bread and warm cider. He ate hungrily and silently. She watched him, also in silence. When he finished, he said, "I would like a room for the night."

"The inn has been closed for months, none of the rooms are made up or fit to sleep in. The storm is very bad, so you may stay here by the fire until it ends," the young woman said.

"But where is the inn keeper?" asked the man, looking about the room.

"The plague has taken both of my parents," the girl replied bravely, but her voice cracked and she became silent and thoughtful.

"I see," said the solider and he too became silent. Minutes later, he fell asleep on the lambskin rug near the fireplace.

**

The young woman stooped to cover him, but stopped long enough to look at his broad shoulders and strong hands. After he was covered, she gazed into his young bearded face.

What makes men go to war, she thought, and turned to her brother. Her brother had been looking with awe at his shining armor, which was drying on the other side of the room. "When I grow up, I will be a great knight and save a king in battle," he said.

The woman stood up and pointed to the door. "Go put the soldier's horse in the stable."

He obeyed surprisingly fast, his sister smiled knowing he was overjoyed at the opportunity to move the strong mount and gaze at the war saddle, lance and shield.

I guess that's how boys are made, ready to go off and fight for a cause, kill or be killed, such a waste. Maybe there will always be wars. She shook her head and her face frowned sadly.

**

The young warrior slept through the night and awoke late the next day. His eyes opened and he realized his locale. Seeing his hostess cooking over the fire, he watched her silently. His heart was alive at the sight of her.

He watched the young boy came in from playing with the shield and the sword, pretending to be a great knight. He smiled at the youngster as he removed his coat and hat, he stomped the mud off his boots. Then the boy came over and sat next to him. The boy asked the soldier, "Where are you going?"

The warrior smiled at the boy's interest in him. He remembered his innocent longing for adventure and faraway lands during his youth. "What is your name, boy?"

"Paul," the boy answered.

The man heaved a sigh. His face tightened and wrinkled in thought. "I have been to the north coast to fight the English."

The knight noticed the girl's eyebrows raised and she turned to face him. He looked up at the beautiful young woman and smiled. "The mistress of the house should certainly know of who is her guest. I am John, of Rheims, second son of the Duke of Rheims. Now allow me to ask my most beautiful hostess her name."

The woman blushed and was visibly shaken. She could not find words.

Her brother answered for her. "That's Julie, my sister."

Julie blushed a shade darker. She bowed low to the ground and signaled to her brother to do the same.

"My lord, how may I please you?" She asked humbly.

"Arise my lady, call me John, you please me with your beauty and your bread. I will see that you are rewarded for your troubles," the young nobleman replied. "If you will allow, I would like some tea when it is ready, and the smell of the baguette waters my mouth."

Tea and bread were served by Julie, who became quite shy and quiet in the presence of the young nobleman. John thought this shyness added to her innocent beauty. He took her hand.

"Do not become withdrawn, your voice is much too sweet not to be heard. Come sit with me by the fire."

The three sat by the fire as the cold wind blew outside. Paul asked John questions about the war, which he wanted to answer, but avoided because a short answer would be incomplete. Finally, seeing that Julie too seemed interested, John agreed to talk about his adventure.

"Peter, my lifelong friend, and I had just returned from a week long hunting trip and we were in high spirits. Two bucks sat carved on our supply horse, our crossbows had proved their match. Saturday would be Peter's twenty-first birthday and there would be quite a feast."

"My older brother, Louis, greeted us with a smile and a laugh. He was always happy and robust. I used to think he never had a care in the world. Being the Duke's oldest, he was groomed for the position he would inherit. He was not the student I was, his math poor, and he never learned Latin. Women and sport were always his first love. This love was repaid in kind, he was never lacking at either."

"Rich news brother," Louis said, with a sparkle in his eyes. "The English have come again. This time we will drive those barbarians into the sea."

"Peter and I looked at each other with open mouths. So we were to be at war. Oh, how lucky to be old enough to go and show our valor and courage, we thought."

"Great excitement had taken over our castle. Visitors from all points of France came and left with messages and news. Battle gear was hastily constructed. Our armaments were repaired, and shields were painted. It seemed the world was never so alive with excitement."

"Peter and I would talk loudly of how we would personally unseat King Henry of England and claim a great ransom for our Duchy and Kingdom. At night I would not be so brave and sleep would come slowly."

"Saturday came and Peter's birthday arrived. A banquet was ordered by my father, who loved Peter like a son. Peter had lost his parents to the Plague and my father brought him into our house to be my youthful mate."

"Everyone was quite happy and excited. The women never looked so beautiful, decorated in the new arrivals from Paris. Venison, game hen, and sweet rolls were laid before us to the delight of our pallets."

"After dinner my father became serious and called all the knights of the castle together. Louis, Peter and I sat in a row on the right of father. The Duchess sat on his left."

"I have received word from the Duke of Orleans. The King has outlawed the Duke of Burgundy, John the Fearless. Burgundy has sided with the English. It is a deep blow to our kingdom. Our king has ordered us to march to join him. Monday we shall depart... I shall see you in church tomorrow gentleman. Now we shall drink and be merry! To Peter on his birthday."

"Peter stood. 'To our most noble duke.' "

"I felt my blood surge with excitement. Monday would not come soon enough for me. I rose 'To Charles, King of the French, we shall drive the English to the sea!' "

"Mother cried when we left on Monday morning at dawn."

"Your mother is said to be the one of the most beautiful women in France," Julie interrupted.

"Ah my mother! Her long brown hair and deep strong brown eyes. Truly she is a magnificent woman. When I was a child, and I did wrong, the look in my mother's eyes would send me to my chamber in shame and I would cry."

"Well, what happened after you departed?" Paul asked impatiently.

"That is all for tonight, Julie quickly interjected, "it is well past the time for you to go to bed."

"Oh, Julie, I'm not tired," Paul begged.

"To bed!" she demanded, stretching to her feet.

Paul looked like he had just lost his best friend. He crawled over to his straw bed and drew his feather quilt over him. Julie, acting more like a mother than a sister, tucked him in and kissed him goodnight. She blessed him and turned to see the young nobleman watching. Her face turned red and she felt her heart pound.

"You are a very good mother to him," John said.

She walked quickly over to the fire and fed it another log. Sparks flew and the red flame rose quickly to consume its new captive as a spider might jump on a fly caught in its web. The embers hid the blood in Julie's face.

John touched her hand and she turned to him. Eyes met and locked his brown to her blue. They could see each other's reflections in their eyes from the glow of the fire. The embrace of the eye was as intense as the heat of the fire. Finally Julie looked away.

"The first flowers of spring would look dull next to your beauty," John said, "Am I so unattractive that you must turn away?"

"Oh sire, no!" Julie responded, "You are truly as fine a man as I ever set eyes upon. But the way you gaze at me makes me humble and blush."

"Come take my hand," he said.

Julie sat next to John and took his blistered battered hand into her soft sleek palm. He noticed her hands were cold while his were finally warm. He gazed at the peasant, her blond clashing with his dark locks. She was like the day and he the night, and like opposite poles of magnets they could not resist the attraction.

John's lips brushed hers, and both felt their blood boil. An embrace, a kiss, a touch, a wish drove them to an exciting new world. The storm raged outside, the fire blazed in the wall stones, and energy exploded into a passion between the two strangers. They made love. When the excitement calmed, Julie cried in John's arms.

"I love you," he said calmly.

"How could you love me? I am but a peasant. Now I am a sinner and you are the son of a duke," Julie said through her tears.

"You are a wonder of the world," he answered the young woman. "In all my life I could never hope to find such peace I have just realized with you."

Julie took his hand and kissed it. A second time they made love. This time the passions were quieter, and more sincere, like a cool breeze on a hot summer's day.

They fell asleep in each other's arms. Morning came to the world. The storm had subsided and a light drizzle fell. John helped with the chores and did much of the heavy work that had been neglected for lack of a man in the house. The three worked hard all day. Evening came and Julie began cooking dinner.

Dinner consisted of beans and bread, both fresh off the hot fire. The three gathered around the fire after dinner and Paul begged John to continue to talk of his adventure.

John started, "We rode early that morning. All of us were very excited about the upcoming battle and new adventure. Five hundred proud knights of Rheims rode double file attended by their squires."

"The duke on his white horse led the way with Louis at his side. Our house's color of the silver fox was held brightly behind them. Peter and I were second in the company."

"Have you seen a nobler army," Peter said, "surely we could take on all of England."

"I readily agreed and we laughed and boasted as we followed the road along the Oise River, toward the Seine and Paris. Ah, Paris! Church spires that reached up toward the heavens, the clunk, clunk of your horse on the cobblestone streets. Bravely, nobly we rode through the wide avenues, sitting high in our saddles. The women of Paris waved from their windows. The young boys greeted us with cheers from every corner. We rode on to the palace of the king."

"I was truly thrilled. I had never seen the king. The duke, my father, had met and counseled with the king's great father, Charles V. Under Charles, the kingdom was well conquered by the English King Edward III had been restored to French rule. The king had died; his son was now the king, Charles VI. None of our family had met him. Rumor had it that he was insane."

"It was afternoon when we arrived at the palace. The Duke of Orleans personally greeted our party. The palace had swelled with people, as a river might swell with water after a great rain. Men in arms were everywhere."

"Welcome fine gentlemen!" Charles, Duke of Orleans greeted us, "Quarters will be provided for your army tonight in the city. Come Rheims and bring your sons, the king awaits."

"I said a quick goodbye to Peter, and rushed to join my father and Louis."

"News is not all good my friends," Orleans began, to our surprise. "The King is not well. He has not been of sound mind for almost a year. We will march for Rouen the second sunrise. I will command the army, while the King will stay in Paris. The Duke of Bourbon will be my chief of staff and you, Rheims, will be his second."

"We had been walking to the banquet hall. Much of the nobility of France was in this room. Our places were pointed out. There were four great tables clothed in white. Benches ran along the sides of each. At the head of the first table there were two thrones, for the King and the Queen. Father was invited to sit at the first table, while Louis and I retreated to the third. We sat and engaged in conversation."

"Trumpets blared, 'Gentlemen the King,' a guard retorted. We all rose as Charles VI, King of France, entered the hall. The queen followed with the prince, Louis, but what attracted my immediate attention was the Princess Katherine. Such beauty, combined with grace, could only become the world once in a century. Helen of Troy and Cleopatra must have been such women. A blanket of light seemed to radiate from her white dress and pale skin. Henry of England, that villain of villains, now threatened to steal her from this court, and demand that she be his bride. Never! I thought."

"The King was boisterous and loud. He laughed loudly, and then retreated to periods of silence. So our King was insane, I thought, at a period when we need him most. I felt disgusted with this man."

"The dinner was delicious. Roast duck with nut bread and stuffing prepared by France's finest chefs. My gaze moved from the King to the Princess, from disappointment to wonder. My brother too, was infatuated with Katherine, as were all the men."

"The next day was spent in conference. Older knights who had fought the English before gave recommendations. A very heavy armor had been constructed to stop arrows of an English longbow. Crossbowmen were picked from hunters from Paris and outlying areas. Excitement jolted through my body, and I slept poorly that night."

"At dawn we rode for Rouen to meet other troops there. Halfway through the day a messenger arrived. The English had landed. I sweltered under my heavy armor. The news seemed to make this hot summer day a little warmer. It was August 13th. Some say thirteen is unlucky. I believed our enemies would be the unlucky ones."

"We took two weeks to reach Rouen. Camp was set along the Seine. Our army was arriving slowly from the far parts of France. The heat in camp was extreme and our movements seemed in slow motion. Everyone was uncomfortably uneasy."

"The first week of September came and we were still not ready to move against invaders. Word came that the garrison of Harfluer had been lost. Still Orleans was not ready to move. I was dismayed by his lack of action, for I was anxious to meet the enemy."

"The end of September came and all was ready. We broke camp and moved north. The heat had not broken and although uncomfortable to our troops, spies learned the English had lost many to sickness and would retreat. I hoped not, I wanted to show those barbarians what it meant to invade our noble France."

"Moving north, our army swelled to over 20,000 men, proud nobility, the flower of the French supported by the best of the hunters with crossbow and men of arms."

"Evening of October 14 our army reached the Somme River near Agincourt. The English were on the other side. Camp was set and a council of war was called. We would wait for the English to attack. When father told me of our plans, I protested. 'Father we outnumber them three to one. Surely victory will be ours if we attack.'

'Let us show them our lances!' Louis agreed.

'No, my good sons. Each day we grow stronger while the English grow weaker. Our supplies are good. The English grow hungry, and if they attack, how will they use their bow?'

"Ten days we waited for the attack. It did not come. Then word was passed to prepare for battle. Finally, I thought with bliss, today was the day I would earn my manhood. As we prepared for battle, an angry wind came from the South. Clouds thickened and it started to rain. Would the rain favor the English or our troops? I did not know."

"We were well organized. The Clugnet de Brabant and Count of Vendome headed the mounted troops. Louis was Vendome's captain. Peter and I were at his side."

"Henry had arranged his army in three divisions, which was traditional for the English. Each division was lined four deep, the last had trenched into the ground."

"Orleans and Bourbon headed our ground forces along with father. Our plan was to let the English attack. Forward they came. My blood rushed, I could hear my heart pound. Gritting my teeth, I found my hand gripping hard at my lance."

"Then the English stopped. We attacked, our crossbowmen going first. The English long bows beat them back before they could get range, and they broke ranks to flee. I didn't believe what happened next. Our ground forces cut off the crossbowmen's retreat and slaughtered them."

"Count Vendome shouted 'Forward,' and we went. My horse flew at full speed."

"The English bowmen let fly and the sky turned black. Arrows fell like rain, horses cried, men screamed. I put my shield up and the impact almost knocked me down. My brave mount bucked in panic. Somehow I was not thrown as another arrow hit my shield. To the right of me I heard a scream. Turning I saw my sweet brother's face turn into a pool of blood."

"'Retreat!' cried Count Vendome as an arrow pierced his armor and entered his chest."

"'Let us be off,' I yelled to Peter, but he was already on the ground lying dead."

"The English then attacked. I fell behind our lines. The battle was over for me. I felt lost and in shock. Dismounting, my stomach let go and I was violently sick."

"The English were on top of our foot soldiers. Because of the heavy armor the French troops were wearing to ward off the longbow arrows, our men had trouble maneuvering in the mud. Charles, Duke of Orleans, fell trying to rally his men. The Duke of Bourbon took an arrow though the neck. The Duke of Rheims was then in command. Father died wielding his sword. I left after that moment and headed home. The battle of Agincourt was over."

The room had become silent. Julie and Paul fought back tears. The pain showed on the young knight's face and the lines on his forehead.

Julie stroked John's hair and he closed his eyes and shivered. He screamed, "Oh God why?" and with a sigh he started to cry. John fell asleep in Julie's arms.

The rain stopped, as a new day started. Sunshine streamed down, shimmering on the silken surface. The tall black oak tree shook off the water dripping on its upper branches as a squirrel scurried up its side. The young knight looked out the front door as he dressed.

"Paul, be so kind as to get me my horse." John turned and walked over to where Julie was waking. He dropped to a knee at her bedside. "I must return home to assume the duties of my new title. I do know we have just met and you are not a lady, but I am the new Duke of Rheims and I will send for you."

He kissed her deeply, knowing that the taste on his lips would have to last for a while. He left his armor with them, mounted his great horse and was off to the southeast. Julie and Paul stood outside and watched him ride away until he dropped off the horizon.

**

The young woman was sure he was gone, just an impossible interlude passing like the wind and rain.

The days turned to nights and months passed. Spring approached and the old oak tree outside the inn budded and young leaves sprouted and started to grow. Julie and Paul were working in the garden planting vegetables to be served in meals at the Inn. Julie stabbed at the soil with a short stick making a row of small holes. Then she would work her way back, sowing the seeds, taking them out of a bag by her belt. Sweat would drip off her bonnet and into her face as the sun reached higher in the sky.

Just before noon they heard the sound of horses coming down the road from the southeast. A coach appeared in the distance with an escort of knights. Julie could see a flag flying from the coach. She squinted into the sunlight at the pennant; it was the coat of arms of the Duke of Rheims! The coach pulled up in front of the Inn. The coachman hopped down and opened the door. The Duke dressed in royal burgundy descended, *her* Duke, John. He smiled looking down at her. Paul and Julie dropped to their knees and bowed.

"Arise my lady," John said, taking her hand. "I know I said I would send for you, but I could not wait to see you again."

He pulled her up from her knees. His arms surrounded her and his lips moved to hers. The kiss was long and deep. The kingdom was about to gain a new duchess. The wind and rain were gone from France, at least for a while. It was spring, and for John, Julie and Paul, the fairy tale would become true.

Fini.

Resiliency

In sports we can find great metaphors for life. Mohammad Ali was amazingly resilient. When he boxed Joe Frazer in the "*Thrila in Manila*" he was pounded by powerful blows. Most men would have been destroyed by the onslaught. Not Ali. He weathered the storm and fought back until he was victorious. He showed the same resiliency in his life. He refused induction into the Army during the Vietnam War because he believed the conflict was unjust. Stripped of his title, and sentenced to jail, he appealed. He won his freedom, and then regained his title in the bout with Frazer.

It is possible that the head shots he took during his boxing career caused the Parkinson's disease problems he now endures. Yet he shows the same determination when facing the disease he did in sports. He has fought back by raising millions of dollars for research and treatment.

So what can we learn from Mohammad Ali's example about dealing with the blows of life? The man love rhyme, so please forgive me this time.

Diseases may strike, which we may not like.
I will try to give some ideas on how to live:

When your body shakes like a butterfly,
 you can still sting like a bee.
Never give up fight for what is right.
When knocked down, get back up win the crown.
Do some good for each neighborhood.
Be the man, help others when you can.
Exercising your body keeps an open lane to your brain.
Eating healthy foods like kelp have been proven to help.
Finding a hobby to keep busy,
will keep your brain from getting dizzy.
Ali always said "I am the greatest."
Have faith in yourself, don't grieve. Believe!
Follow this advice about being resilient;
It will help to keep your mind brilliant.

Colleen and I vacationed in Italy the summer of 2013.

37. Pre-dawn Pasitono, Italy 2013

Early morning light touches me like a lover away too long.

The blue-grey sea lies flat, becalmed after a week of churning

turbulence. Clouds hide the rising sun dulling the pastels

walls and terracotta roofs of hotels and houses that hang

precariously from the eroding limestone cliffs. Black sand and

pebble beach enriched by Vesuvius' volcanic eruptions two

centuries earlier looks up with a wink and a smile.

"Come play with me," she says seductively.

I answer, "Be patient, it's early. I'm in no hurry. I will explore

your offerings slowly, like wine that grows from your

hillsides."

Positono, small quiet is a refuge from the barbarian hordes that have invaded Rome, Florence and Venice. There is no "Pox-Romania" in the treasure trove of modern Italy. Goths, Visigoths and Huns could not rival the torrents of tourists sacking the cities looking for artifacts to plunder. It was impossible to saver anything of value or beauty as the multitudes compete for a spot before each historical wonder. The transition from night to day is almost complete. Looking down at the beautiful beckoning Mediterranean Sea, I take a breath, pause to reflect on the gifts of genius that the Italian ancestors offered the world.

38. *Reflections on Rome*
Or what I learned from Uncle Walt
May 2013

I loved Rome but I could not avoid thinking that it was too much Roman Catholic and not enough Ancient Rome. I wanted more history. The Coliseum and the Forum were cool but they just wetted my appetite so I am offering an alternative to the traditional Vatican and Church tour. Not that the Pope's place wasn't amazing and we know the Church could always use more tourist money. All that art work is astonishing material. Don't miss it.

But I want more Roman Empire stuff. OK so here's my proposal, drum roll please:

"CAESARLAND"- A place to make Ancient Rome come alive:

I. Refurbished Roman Coliseum complete with:

   a. Gladiator fights (OK is the 21st Century-no killing.)

   b. Chariot Racing (Gambling encouraged-look what it did for the Indian tribes.)

   c. Olympic style sporting events (I know that was Greek but close enough.)

II. Roman Forumland with recreated scenes from history like Julius Caesar being stabbed.

III. Roman legion battles including Rome vs. Carthage complete with Hannibal's Elephants.

IV. Real Roman Orgies (Adults Only) Don't worry Mom and Dad, free babysitting.

V. Plundering- A visit to the Roman shopping district

VI. We end the day with the Vesuvius mountain volcano recreation spectacular.

I know you think this is really a stupid idea. Well people thought Disneyland was crazy at one time. Look at the lira that place pulls in. Anything that brings history alive is alright by me.

After all I went to Rome to Praise Caesar not to bury him.

39. *Democracy's Dissolution*

April 2013

My twenty-year old son refuses to vote.

he believes all politicians are corrupt

it's hard to argue with his logic

when it takes millions or billions

getting elected to a job that pays thousands.

it's totally legal to accept the campaign funds

if one doesn't let it influence the vote in congress

obvious irony does not lie

just the system and the candidates

all these millions does not make *cents*.

40. Excerpt from: *The Penngrove Ponderosa* – *Surviving the social and sexual revolution in Northern California, a short novel.*

From Chapter 3

September is usually the warmest month in the Bay Area. But the day of the fall equinox the sky filled with fog, chilling any underdressed, unaware California tourist to the bone. Laura Goldman blew into town like a winter storm. To Don and his friends, his big sister was a ray of sunshine.

No one knew she was coming. Laura had taken a greyhound bus across the country and arrived in Oakland wearing just shorts and a tee-shirt. By the time local transit deposited her to the Telegraph Avenue apartment she was freezing. She leaned on the door buzzer. Wilkes answered, "Who's there?"

"John Booth, you get me out of this cold windy fog."

"Who is it?"

"Laura."

"Laura who?"

"Laura Goldman, you ditz."

"Holy shit!" He hit the buzzer and let Don's big sister into the apartment.

Laura came into the flat grabbed a throw blanket and folded

her lengthy slender 23 year-old body into a living room chair. Her long brown hair fell down to her shoulders and her brown eyes sparkled as she asked, "Where is my little brother?"

"Out working, he got a temporary job selling Fuller Brush products door to door in San Leandro. Did he tell you we are planning to stay here awhile?"

"Yea, I was wondering if I could crash with you guys a little while. I made some plans to go to graduate school just north of here."

"I'm sure you could crash here for a while. What college? Where?"

"Have you heard of Sonoma State College? It's about fifty miles north. They have a great humanistic psychology program. You know Don dropped out of Yale last spring, hated economics, I thought he might want to join me, try psych or something. What about you?"

"I never went to college, had a pretty good job as an apprentice plumber, good money, union, but I couldn't see working in Queens the rest of my life. I've got some money in the bank so I just came along for the ride. Don't know if college is my thing, but I'm ready to check out some new stuff, if you know what I mean."

"Yeah, sure, me too, that's why I'm here." She shivered a little. The cold made her nipples hard noticeable against the cotton fabric of her shirt. Laura giggled, noticing that Wilkes was glancing lower than her eyes during their conversation. "John Wilkes Booth, are you checking out my boobs?"

His face flushed red, "To tell you the truth Laura they are not hard to notice."

"I'm wet and cold and I need a hot shower." Laura pulled her clingy tee shirt over her head, her breasts with her cold hard nipples peeking out at the younger man. She chuckled and headed to the bathroom as her hips swayed walking away from him. She said, "I remember when you used to look at me when I was a senior and you were a sophomore. Keep those thoughts Wilkes, you just might get lucky yet."

The bathroom door closed, the water started and all Wilkes could do was sit there and say, "Wow!"

A minute later he heard her yell from the shower, "Hey, John Wilkes, there's a spot on my back I can't reach."

41. *I want to be in that Number*

October 23, 2013

Spent five days in the Big Easy,
Southern oasis of culture
surrounded by swamp gators,
snap-turtles and rednecks.

Somehow the city
stays stationary in time,
Bayou jazz overtaken by rock and roll.
She once was the queen, Southern bell of the ball.
A touch of gray mixes rich brunette locks,
crow's feet edge the lovely brown eyes.

Still no city can match her ethnic beauty,
fine mix of
Creole, Cajun, Spanish, African and Antebellum American.
Or the taste of her cooking:
crawdads, shrimp, turtle, crab, lobster, filet mignon combine
in a rich hot red pepper gumbo sauce, served over buttered
grits.
Ya'll, the ol' girl sure knows how to throw a party,
as the Saints go marching on.

42. 2125 AD

This advertisement is the first thing I hear as I come out
of my induced coma. I am a twenty-first century man
wakening up in the twenty-second century.
The United States, which by 20 52 included Canada and
Mexico, returned to manned space flight after The United
Arab States started a space program. There is nothing like a
cold war to induce space innovation. The Arabs and all their
oil money decided to explore space and wanted to land on one
of Saturn's or Jupiter's moons to look for natural resources.
Most commodities on Earth were getting scarce.

The last thing I can remember before my attached antenna brain pack picked up this ad was being on an experimental flight to Titan, Saturn's biggest moon. My robot companion, Mercury, named after the first U.S. manned space ships, warned, "Dave something is seriously wrong with the space ship, fuel has been leaking and I am going to implement emergency alternative 'foxtrot.'"

"Are you sure Mercury, that's a pretty radical program?" I said. (It would mean all other options for safe returns to Earth were not available. I would be put into an induced coma, inside a life supporting bubble the ships other programs would be shut down and I would drift into space until NASA Control could find a way to save me. This alternative was experimental. While this program had been built into all of this type of spacecraft, it had never been used and was the last resort for a desperate situation.)

"Yes, Dave that is the only way to save you, sorry. Good luck Dave. You will be asleep in 10, 9, 8, 7, 6, 5, 4, 3, 2..."

**

Consciousness comes to me slowly in this new century. The advertisement unnerves me as I struggled to awake. Hospital buzzers sounded and a team of workers come running to my aid.

"Welcome to 2125 the strange looking man said with what I think is a smile," I am Jordish-Michael number 7062, your head doctor. You are a lucky man. We found you spacecraft drifting outside the solar system and your central nervous system was still alive after we pulled your craft back to earth. Our stem cell technology replaced all your damaged body systems. "The "man" talking to me had a humongous sized head. His skin was bright green. He hand had seven fingers including three dexterous thumbs.

"Thank you," was all I could manage to say, totally unnerved and shocked realizing I had been drifting in space for 83 years.

**

I learn quickly about the 22nd century society. War and disease were a thing of the past. The new models of humanity have been genetically programed to get along. They were amazingly intelligent. Mental illness was defeated by genetic engineering.

With all these advancements, I feel something is missing. The architecture, dance, music of this culture are beautiful but lacking in something. What is it? I struggle to figure it out.

Then after many 22nd Century novels are beamed to my cerebrum, I realize what is missing. Without the "crazy" genotype, we have lost the rebels. These modern "humans" are genetically programed to get along, go with the flow. True innovation is sacrificed. Radical change in style is stifled. There are no Kurt Vonnegut, Steven King, H. G. Wells or Susan B. Anthony types of people in this environment. Without mutation and natural selection I figure humanity is stuck in a nondescript treadmill.

Unfortunately, I now have other more immediate and personal things to worry about. I have to somehow get out of this God forsaken hospital. But I'm trapped. My new bones are not yet hardened enough to walk. Jordish-Michael number 7062 has planned to do surgery on me tomorrow, modernizing me. I will be getting an antenna implanted and will have my "unnecessary" penis removed.

October, 2013
Happy Halloween!

This story was my first attempt at Science Fiction. The ad came to me first like it was beamed to me from the future. Do you think it could have actually have come to me from... no couldn't be.

Falling

September 2012

The Big Apple was all lit up, waiting for the ball to drop.
When she entered the party,
the rest of the room went out of focus.
Her blue green eyes sparkled like the lights
aglow on Broadway.

I was looking for a good time.
She was looking for... I did not know.
Her accent was Russian, giving an impression of intrigue.

We came together,
North and South Pole type of magnetism,
lustful flirtation, frolic, fun
a bathtub full of champagne.

Manic hunger lurked inside her.
Every trace of passion spent.
I slept holding on, enchanted, exhausted.

We both knew I would leave with the sunrise,
back to California.
She promised to visit, refused to say goodbye.

How could I know she had one leg over the balcony?
Depression found her like some evil stalker.

She fell out of my dreams and into my nightmares,
forever falling, falling, never hitting the ground.

That was a downer; let's go to with something lighter:

December Sunrise

Rays of light pokes its head up from the southeast,
ground's frost gleams as beams reflect a dim radiance.
Cold nips at my nose like a teething puppy.
Fog holds onto the hills refusing to let go.

As his royal highness, the sun god arrives, winning
the battle against the long winter night,
hundreds of starlings take wing
chased by a single white hawk.

The birds fly in flow of golden glow formations
like an acid inspired light show at a 60's
Grateful Dead Concert,
moving with a grace that would make
the Blue Angels green with envy
sky suddenly so alive, it takes my breath away,
into awesome mist.

The prompt that day in my writing group was: Write your own eulogy. This might be a good place to end.

43. *Goodbye and Thanks for Coming*

Today's date?

Sorry I had to go. You're probably wondering where I went. It's a secret we are not allowed to tell. Many of you know I was a skeptic when it came to an infinite afterlife. One of reasons for the skepticism was that no one ever talked about the infinite before-life. So, l created a little of my heaven in no particular order.
Heaven is:
when my wife and son are happy.
teaching, really teaching and students learning.
skiing a great run at the top of Beaver Bowl at Alpine Meadows.
reading a great book.
writing a good book.
the fog receding from the grape vines of Saint Helena on a beautiful summer's day.
Yosemite just after the snow fall, enveloped in powder.
playing street football when I was ten years old with leaves falling off the trees.
spending the summer day playing ball with my buddies as a kid then dipping my face in a cold tub of water.
falling in love.
my dogs' friendships.
sunset over a beautiful beach.
snorkeling in a pool of fish.
catching a wave.

whacking a baseball over the fence.
playing tennis with a good friend..
an evening with good friends or family.
watching the perfect movie.
sailing under the Golden Gate and knowing I was home.
when I was a teenager and a beautiful girl walks by in a bikini
eating an ice cream cone.
sharing the ice cream cone with her the nest day.
my first kiss.
when with a friend, something is so funny that I laugh until
tears and snot runs down my face.
good health, no pain.
people who do good.
watching wild animals run free.
spring flowers in bloom, autumn leaves.
The beautiful earth…
I would go on, but you get it. Enjoy every day.

Books by Nathaniel Robert Winters: all on Amazon or Kindle

Rumors about my Father and other stories: A novella/memoir about prohibition, the Depression, W.W. II and other issues of life in the 20th Century.

The Legend of Heath Angelo: a novella about the man who started the first Nature Conservancy Preserve in California

No Place for a Wallflower: a novella/memoir about Iola Hitt's World War II experience.

Finding Shelter from the Cold: a young adult to adult novel about Ice Age wolves and their interaction with man.

The Adventures of the Omaha Kid: a novel about sports, romance and finding a place to call home.

The Penngrove Ponderosa-Surviving the sexual and social revolution of the 70's in Northern California, a novel

This book is dedicated to America's teachers. Embattled and underappreciated they work hard to feed the minds and hearts of today's youth. It is a job of love but not easy. I'm proud of my thirty years in the classroom and sports fields.

Acknowledgments: I would like to thank the Solstice Writers Group of Saint Helena. Their guidance brought out my inner poet.

25141487R00074

Made in the USA
Charleston, SC
21 December 2013